The Heart & Soul of I

How Lean Management aligns

with the better angels of our nature

to create extraordinary results

Bill Waddell

2015

The Heart and Soul of Manufacturing

Copyright © 2015 by Bill Waddell

Cover Art and Contents by Bill Waddell (www.bill-waddell.com)

Edited and published by William J. Waddell. South Bend, IN. 2015

ISBN13: 978-1514188187

ISBN10: 151418818X

First Printing: June 2015

"For it seems to me that the first responsibility of a man of faith is to make that faith really part of his own life, not by rationalizing it but by living it."

Thomas Merton

No Man is an Island

This book is not about religion, and I make no attempt to convert the reader to any particular faith. Instead I am looking to convert the reader to a different understanding of management. My assumption is that the vast majority of people working in management roles already have a sense of purpose to their life that recognizes that there are things more important than themselves and their material needs. They know, either in the precise words of their faith, or at least at a gut level, that they have an obligation to serve others – that, 'he who dies with the most toys' does not, in fact, win.

Three fourths of Americans profess to be Christians, and almost 90% of us profess to believe in the existence of a higher power – a Creator. In spite of our collective belief in something greater than ourselves, and the common principle among all faiths that we are here to serve God and our fellow human beings, we live in an increasingly secular culture. Many, if not all, of us who believe in God struggle to live our faith in an American society that is more and more centered on the material; and we struggle to raise our children as we would like to in the cultural onslaught that would have us believe that money and possessions should be the focus of worship.

Nowhere is this gap between our inner spiritual values and the values of society in sharper contrast than in the business world. People such as Jack Welch and Steve Jobs are lionized on the basis of the staggering wealth they accumulated for themselves and for their investors, but both were dogged by track records of questionable treatment of the people who contributed greatly to the creation of all of that wealth. Welch was known as "Neutron Jack" within GE, named for the neutron bomb that was designed to kill people while leaving buildings intact. He earned this nickname based on his track record of causing hundreds of thousands of GE employees to lose their jobs as he replaced them not because they performed poorly or did not work hard enough, but because people were available in faraway, often oppressed corners of the world who would work cheaper. Similarly, Jobs was dogged with nagging questions about the working conditions in China where better than a dozen poorly paid young workers opted to commit suicide rather than face another day in the factories making Apple products.

If pursuit of wealth is the #1 goal in life then there are few people more successful than Welch and Jobs, and the large number of executives who, while not anointed with 'CEO of the Decade' accolades have amassed similar personal fortunes, but have also done so at the cost of enormous misery in the lives of thousands of employees, for their families and for the communities in which they once operated.

The target audience of this book is not such leaders. I strongly suspect their minds are firmly made up as to their priorities. Rather, it is the managers who work in the bowels of companies led by such people. They find themselves having to contribute to the management processes that result in so much human damage, but cannot see an alternative if they are to gain favor with their bosses and bring home the paychecks needed to support their own families. I know of so many such people who go home at the end of each week conflicted, having received the approval of the boss but troubled by their conscience, a nagging feeling that relegating good people, God's creations, to 'headcount' and working to eliminate their jobs is not right.

And the target audience includes the leaders and managers of the thousands of smaller and medium sized companies who are bombarded with the message from the so-called experts that they must emulate the practices of these leaders if their business is to be successful. They too struggle with the conflict. They need to be profitable in order for the company to remain healthy, but the 'headcount' they are told to minimize and the jobs they are urged to outsource are jobs held by their friends and neighbors, the people in their own communities who they know to be good and decent folks. They also have this inner conflict between their imperative need for financial success and the greater need to be true to their core beliefs – their faith. They genuinely love people and believe they can do enormous good, but are compelled to create an adversarial relationship with those very same people

This book has good news for that target audience. There is no need for the conflict. The conflict is caused by a misguided, antiquated set of management practices that are not only unnecessary, but have never been too terribly effective, largely driven by accounting theories that are grossly misleading in their failure to direct management to the true drivers of costs and sources of profitability. The solution is a different and well proven approach to management – the principles of lean management that seems to be one of manufacturing management's best kept secrets.

Many potential readers will stop reading as soon as they see the word 'lean'. They think they know what lean is and have tried it, and learned that it doesn't work, or have come to see it as a collection of tools on the factory floor with little bearing on the management of the business. To those people I would suggest that, if you think lean doesn't work it is most likely because you understand it in a very limited way – as techniques to be used in support of the same old business model. I ask that you give me just a few more minutes of your time, stick with me for just a few chapters, and see if perhaps there isn't a dimension to lean beyond that which you thought you knew. I strongly suspect you will find a whole new world – one in which companies are managed by practices and processes and fueled by an approach to accounting the likes of Jack Welch and Steve Jobs never contemplated.

The people leading and working in these companies routinely realize profit margins most big companies rarely see (and only then through accounting manipulations and numbers games), and more important, their leaders never have to rationalize or apologize to anyone. Their managers have no inner conflicts. They have found and sharpened a way of managing the business that not only aligns with their faith, but uses their faith as the driving principle that brings financial success and security to everyone involved.

Bill Waddell

INTRODUCTION

For close to thirty years I have been involved with lean manufacturing – since even before the term was coined, in fact, and during that time I have had the chance to meet and work with most of the well-known experts, have come to know many successful company lean leaders, and I've seen quite a few lean failures. The question that is most often asked is 'what is the key to success?'; 'What are the common attributes of successful leaders of the transformation to Toyota-like success?'

During that time I have grown in my own thinking from seeing lean as an exciting new set of tools to use on the factory floor and in the supply chain, to an all-encompassing business and economic model, to what it truly is: All of the above driven by and centered on a powerful and rare organizational culture. To the often asked question, "What is the role of leadership in a lean transformation?" the answer is, "To be the passionate believer in and driver of that culture".

The key to that culture; the common attribute among those who realize success beyond their wildest expectations is management building, leading and continually strengthening a culture driven by a belief in a higher purpose than simply making money. Usually that means a strong belief in God, a conviction that the leaders and the organization don't make money simply for its own sake, but in order to make their corner of the world a better place. They believe they were put on this earth for reasons other than to pursue their own selfish purposes, and feel a strong sense of responsibility for the people in their sphere of influence.

That statement was huge, and it makes all the difference. When the company exists with an ending objective of making money then it is bound by no principles – money has no morals. But when making money is the second last step – the final objective is something else – something to be done with the money that is good – the entire company pursues profits within a moral code that changes everything.

This conviction that there are things more important than themselves doesn't necessarily translate into required participation in a formal religion although most do. Nor does it mean belief in a higher power as defined by any particular faith. What it means is a sense of responsibility for the welfare of others, an internal moral code that transcends profits, a belief in the inherent goodness of people and a genuine respect for others simply because those 'others' are human beings and, therefore, deserving of respect. It means a belief that we were put on this earth to serve, rather than to take.

Some time ago Jim Huntzinger, the founder and president of Lean Frontiers, and I began a running conversation that began with a casual chat in which we realized that we had come to lean for business purposes – a way to do our jobs in manufacturing more efficiently – but had stayed with it, became passionate about it, and devoted our careers to it because it also provided us with a way of working that aligned with our deeper moral principles.

In the Book of Galatians, Paul asks, "*Am I now trying to win the approval of human beings, or of God? Or am I trying to please people? If I were still trying to please people, I would not be a servant of Christ.*" That is really the core question for all people of all faiths. The problem with working for an organization – any organization – is that financial security and providing for one's family depends on pleasing people – the boss, in particular. When that which pleases the boss is also pleasing to

God, or if God is neutral on the subject, all is well. Too often, however, the things that are defined as 'successful" and pleasing to the boss cause a bit of discomfort. We have an underlying uneasiness that continually pressuring subordinates, demanding more and more, laying people off, taking work away from long term suppliers, closing plants – the things we find ourselves having to do (or at least participate in) wouldn't be too terribly pleasing to the Almighty.

The cut throat world of business, and especially manufacturing over the last thirty years, has become centered on the negative: Laying off good people in pursuit of lower headcounts, closing plants and moving the work to China, decimating entire small towns across America, and bankrupting small suppliers by abruptly terminating long relationships and replacing them with cheaper foreign sources. It is hard to be a party to such decisions and still go home at the end of the day and reconcile our work with our inner moral compass. It seems insufficient – hypocritical, in fact – to devote time on the weekends to charitable causes and in efforts to help the community, often through our church, when the folks on the receiving end of that charity need it because we helped to eliminate their jobs.

Jim and I were inspired in those early conversations by the manor in which lean represents a completely opposite approach. It is a set of tools and practices within an over-arching business model and driven by a culture that embraces and empowers people, treating the loss of someone's job as a complete failure of management. It drives companies to long term relationships with suppliers, and the more difficult it is for a supplier to compete, the more urgent it is for the company to embrace that supplier. And lean is completely customer focused.

The magic and power of lean is that it has the potential to drive profits to levels not even dreamed of under the old model. At the same time it enabled both of us to achieve the manufacturing success we desired, confident that we were doing so in a manner that not only aligned with but actually was supported by our personal values. We didn't have to change who we were and how we act when we turned the calendar page from Sunday to Monday. It provided a livelihood that Jim and I appreciated as one that enabled us to answer Paul's question with the comfort that what we were doing was pleasing to both God and man. Eventually those conversations turned into this book.

As a young, very junior person rising up through the manufacturing ranks I would have pangs of conscience when layoff notices were posted, feeling deep empathy for the young men and women who were laid off, envision them having to go home and give their young spouse the bad news, and then spending sleepless nights worrying about how they were going to pay the bills and take care of their families. But I could see the senior managers who I knew personally to be good and decent men looking seemingly impervious to such feelings of remorse.

I thought that was just how business was. You just had to separate your feelings from the job, set your personal sense of right and wrong aside, be tough, and do what the numbers dictated for the good of the stockholders whose money, after all, we were spending. I assumed that after so many decades of management evolution smarter people than I had worked through all of these ethical issues and conflicts and had arrived at a consensus that it was the right way to operate.

And then I came across Toyota with its nearly perfect track record of providing lifetime employment to its workers – and making an awful lot of money at the same time. And one by one I encountered at first a trickle, then a stream and now a fairly wide river of other companies doing the same thing. And I have come to know with absolute certainty that there is no need for any conflict between moral principles and good, profitable management.

This book is not about religion, and I want to be the first to say that I am perhaps the least qualified person on the planet to write about that sensitive subject. By practice I am a Catholic, but not a particularly good one. I am deeply flawed but I believe in God and I have been blessed with family, friends and associates who have helped me stumble along the path to try to become a better man. And I appreciate that those people come from many different faiths and belief systems.

I cannot state strongly enough that it is not necessary for manufacturing success that one be a follower of any religion. The founders of SC Johnson prove that point. They have been a highly principled, and simultaneously successful company since their founding in 1866 with never a layoff in all that time. Hebert F. Johnson, Sr. once said, *"The goodwill of people is the only enduring thing in any business. It is the sole substance. The rest is shadow."* Focus on that North Star seems to have enabled the company to thrive through two world wars and the Great Depression without having to compromise on its higher ideals.

Yet by all accounts the early Johnsons had a rather contentious relationship with the local Presbyterian Church, and were hardly regular church goers. They could not be called particularly religious men, but there is no questioning that they were highly principled men with faith in God and a strong sense of a higher purpose for the company than simply making money for its own sake.

So it's not about what church, mosque or synagogue you visit, or if you even visit one at all. It is about believing in a higher purpose for your life and career.

I know to be a fact that manufacturing management is largely comprised of people like me. They are good people who want to do their jobs well, but also want to treat people well and they want to know that their careers are resulting in more than just their own paychecks, they want to have a positive impact on the world around them and especially on the people around them.

The purpose for this book is to send the message to those people that it is possible to do both. That the very best aspect of lean manufacturing – truly deep cultural lean – is that it provides a path for good people to combine the crafts of their trade with their moral code; to be good manufacturers *because* they are good people, rather than feeling they must either be good manufacturers *or* good people.

CHAPTER 1: *Rooted in a Higher Power*

In the late 1980's Toyota was outperforming and thoroughly mystifying American manufacturing management with what was then known as 'JIT'. This 'system' used cards called 'kanbans' rather than computers with complicated MRP software. Impossibly high quality levels were being routinely achieved. The whole thing was shrouded in Japanese terms like kaizen and gemba, and serious men with odd sounding names like Taiichi Ohno and Shigeo Shingo were the driving architects. Perhaps most radically different from the factories of their American competitors was Toyota's approach to people. Toyota shop floor production workers were neck deep in solving problems and saving money; they were empowered to pull a cord and stop the production lines; and perhaps most amazingly were never laid off. Employees at Toyota had jobs for life.

Trying to figure out exactly what Toyota was doing progressed from a matter of intellectual curiosity to a matter of considerable urgency as Toyota increasingly won over customers, gobbled up U.S. market share and made a lot of money in the process. Explanations included the Japanese government manipulating the currency – which was true, but the Toyota juggernaut continued even after the Reagan administration took action to level the playing field. Toyota had beaten the Americans to the market with smaller, more fuel efficient cars – also true, but once again, Toyota's inroads weren't slowed in the least when the Americans finally came out with small, high mileage cars of their own.

The explanation that had the most long term traction was national culture. According to the Harvard Business Review in 1991, *"Knowledgeable visitors to Japan reported that the manufacturing excellence they saw there seemed rooted in the Japanese culture itself -- attention to detail, individual sacrifice for collective goals, order, neatness."*

This explanation – that it was a uniquely Japanese thing – would have been a good one had it held up. It would have taken the Americans off the hook for their inability to mimic Toyota's results. But it didn't hold up. Through the 1990's and into the 2000's a number of Japanese companies acted and performed very much like American companies. Sony, for instance, outsourced large chunks of manufacturing to cheap labor places and moved into businesses far from its core; and laid off workers by the tens of thousands. This was hardly reflective of the way Toyota did business.

And at the same time a few American companies were able to adopt the Toyota model. Today companies such as Barry-Wehmiller – the St Louis based packaging machine builder - and ATC – a trailer manufacturer in northern Indiana – are every bit as impressive as Toyota (albeit on a smaller scale) in terms of culture and employee engagement, as well as financial results. These companies, and hundreds – perhaps thousands – like them pursue 'lean manufacturing' in a very holistic way. That is to say, they don't merely adopt the various shop floor tools and techniques of the Toyota System, but place every bit as much emphasis on the people centered culture of Toyota.

Most telling, Toyota plopped a factory down in the heart of America – Georgetown, Kentucky – and filled it with workers as American as apple pie and deployed the same methods and the same culture with just as much success as when their factories were located in Japan and filled with Japanese workers.

With undeniable evidence that being Japanese doesn't guarantee manufacturing success, and being American doesn't preclude it, the secret to the sauce must come from something other than ethnicity or national heritage – and it does.

The studies of Toyota have focused on the factories and the techniques developed by the key architects of their processes – guys like the aforementioned Taiichi Ohno who ran production at Toyota during their ascendency, and Shigeo Shingo, who was an industrial engineering consultant to Toyota. Digging deeper, however, one finds a very remarkable fact. Toyota has been guided by a set of five precepts laid out long ago by its founder, Sakichi Toyoda, and diligently followed by succeeding generations of leaders from the Toyoda family. They are currently stated as:

1. *Be contributive to the development and welfare of the country by working together, regardless of position, in faithfully fulfilling your duties.*

2. *Be ahead of the times through endless creativity, inquisitiveness and pursuit of improvement.*

3. *Be practical and avoid frivolity.*

4. *Be kind and generous; strive to create a warm, homelike atmosphere.*

5. *Be reverent, and show gratitude for things great and small in thought and deed.*

Inspiring enough as written, but even more powerful when the watered down, Americanized translation of precept #5 was translated more honestly, more literally by Toyota expert and former resident of Japan, Jon Miller: *"Venerate the Gods and Buddhas and live a life of gratitude and repayment for kindness."*

Why did Toyota water it down? Marketing probably. So as not to send a message to any intolerant potential Toyota buyers that they *"venerate the Gods and Buddhas"*. Perhaps they don't want to align themselves with any particular faith – especially one considerably outside of the American mainstream.

In fact, this faith centered approach to the business is the common thread. The pre-eminent American 'lean manufacturer' – one that is every bit Toyota's equal in its people-centered culture, as well as its ability to make a lot of money along the way is Barry-Wehmiller. The chief architect of the Barry-Wehmiller business model and its extraordinary culture is CEO Bob Chapman. He traces the origins of his journey to make the

> *""We measure success by the way we touch the lives of people."*
> *This fundamental belief rests at the*
> *heart of our Guiding Principles of Leadership. We believe that any leadership decision can be weighed*
> *against this statement and that we can measure true success by the way we are able to make a sustained,*
> *positive impact on our team members and their families, our suppliers and customers, our communities, our capital providers,*
> *and our shareholders.*
>
> **Barry-Wehmiller corporate website.**

company what it became to *"divine inspiration"* that occurred while he listened to a rector in an Episcopal church. Bob talks with great passion of a sense of stewardship for the blessings he has received when he describes the Barry-Wehmiller business model and his role in it.

This same view of business leadership as one of great responsibility for the welfare and quality of life of the people engaged in the business – mostly employees but suppliers, customers, folks in the community as well – is present in the thinking of others. ATC's Steve Brenneman, a graduate of

Eastern Mennonite University believes in and is driven by his faith and the Mennonite principles of Christian stewardship; the belief that all men are inherently good; and that he has a great responsibility for the stewardship of the inherently good people who work for his company, buy his products, and rely on him to positively impact the lives of many folks in tiny Nappanee, Indiana where his factories are.

> *"If our employees' kids have to be on subsidized lunches and things like that, it's not successful, not to me."*
>
> **Steve Brenneman, CEO Aluminum ATC Trailers**

And there is Greg Wahl, third generation CEO of the Wahl Clipper Company. Like Toyota, ATC and Barry-Wehmiller, Wahl doesn't lay people off, is driven by lean, and, most notably, is very, very profitable. To the outsider, the Wahl Company and the Wahl family have become synonymous with Catholic education in Sterling, Illinois – their home town. They have almost single-handedly paid for the Catholic elementary and high schools and have poured enormous sums into upgrading and enhancing those schools once built. Those inside the company, however, are more keenly aware of the fierce passion with which Greg drives the company to take care of the feelings and experience of each of the thousands of employees and his absolute commitment to assuring that the company is a huge positive contributor to the community. He lives the company principles of family as the center.

The examples are endless. The common thread among the great lean companies is faith in a higher principle, and a sense of responsibility for the people and material resources upon whom the company relies, and the people who, in turn, rely on the company. The particular brand of faith is not important, whether it is the Nichiren Buddhism of Sakichi Toyoda and his descendants, the protestant Christianity of Bob Chapman, the

Anabaptist Mennonite faith of Steve Brenneman, the Catholicism of Greg Wahl or that of Muslims in the pursuit of excellence and quality because they believe that those are the things that please Allah; the underlying principle is always the same.

And sometimes the leader has little more than a deep, gut feel for his faith, as in the case of Timberland CEO Jeff Schwartz who said of moving his production out of China because worker rights were being trampled on in the process of making Timberland's shoes, "*I can't show you the scripture that relates to the rights of a worker, but I can show you text that insists upon treating others with dignity. It says in the Hebrew Bible one time that you should love your neighbor as yourself, but it says dozens of times that you shall treat the stranger with dignity.*"

This is not to say that faith based leadership guarantees the results of a Toyota or a Wahl Clipper. There are numerous examples of faith driven leaders who have failed or have felt the need to take actions that run counter to the people-centric approach of Barry-Wehmiller and the rest. Tyson Chicken comes to mind.

"*Founder John Tyson speaks openly about his Christian beliefs, and the company's core values say that it 'strive(s) to honor God' and 'be a faith-friendly company'*," according to BusinessWeek. Yet Tyson Foods laid off workers in 2006 and again in 2007 in order to "*cut expenditures*" and "*improve efficiencies*". There is no questioning the sincerity of John Tyson's faith and his commitment to people. After all, the company has deployed some "*128 part-time chaplains (including both Protestant and Catholic Christians and Muslim Imams) in 78 Tyson plants.*"

No, the problem at Tyson is most likely the one most managers who have been trained in traditional practices face: A seeming contradiction between principles and profit. There is a belief – a misguided belief, as the excellent lean companies demonstrate – that to be a profitable businessperson one must leave his or her faith at the door when coming to work. We have been taught that there is no room for sentimentality in the rough and tumble of business; that business requires toughness and hard actions; and those actions *"might include, for instance, laying people off, cutting workers' compensation and benefits, outsourcing jobs to lower-wage regions, forcing suppliers to cut their prices, forcing communities to cut a company's taxes, violating safety or environmental regulations, and much more"*, decries Portland State professor emeritus H. Thomas Johnson.

The point is that we have been led to believe in the Godfather principle: That business is business, and not to be confused with personal beliefs and feelings. As Bob Chapman said, we have come to think we have to put a mask on when we go to work – to be someone other than the person who sat in the church, synagogue or mosque, or simply reveled in the glory of God's creations over the weekend, and then left all of that behind when Monday morning rolled around and it was time to banish the personal for the sake of business.

The aim of this book is to spread the good news – that "The Godfather" is no place to get a business education; that your college professors were wrong, and that business not only doesn't have to be a cold, numbers driven place; that it can be every bit as profitable – even more so – when it is managed in a manner wholly consistent with your highest level values and beliefs.

Most important, there are many, many managers who spend their careers with an unsettling feeling that the things they are compelled to do are just not right. They know that people are not 'headcount' and that no matter how much shareholder value they create they can't really square the way it was done with the message of love and stewardship they hear in church, or know in their gut to be the right way to live. They think they have no choice. Like Tyson, they think they must be either faith driven or efficient, but can't see a way to be both.

We have come to rationalize the stark contrasts between the love and generosity inherent in the American spirit – we are far and away the most generous and giving nation on the planet – with the way we feel we must conduct business. There is the 'good of the whole' storyline: 'As much as we don't want to and as much as we truly care for the 500 people working in the plant in Anytown, we have to close it down and lay them off if we are going to protect the livelihood of the 4,500 people working in our other locations.'

And there is the 'moral obligation to the shareholders' idea: 'It is not our money. It is theirs. We have no right to impose our moral judgments on them and we have a primary responsibility to them to protect their money and provide them with the greatest possible return'.

We say those things, but they don't really ring true deep down. The layoff notices are posted and whole towns are decimated. People we have worked with for years are left to fend for themselves and their families with limited prospects even though they personally did everything we as managers ever asked of them; but at the end of the week we go home with a hollow feeling in the pit of our stomach, knowing that our moral rationalizations for what was done in the spirit of business would sound rather unconvincing if we were confronted by our maker and asked about our actions.

When Emerson wrote that most men live lives of quiet desperation he may well have been describing most of the managers of American businesses. On the weekends they attend church, pour time and money into their communities doing everything from coaching little league to teaching Sunday school, then go back to work on Monday to do work that rubs all of those loving, humanitarian instincts the wrong way.

We all know that our day will come; that sooner or later someone will dig a hole in the ground and lower what is left of us down into it, and then someone will have something to say about our lives. We know that what will be said won't include anything about budgets met, profit margins achieved or how much we enhanced shareholder value. All that will matter is how we touched the lives of people – were the folks who came into contact with us better or worse off for the experience? For many people who spent their careers in management that unsettled feeling comes from the knowledge that we were tasked with leading many people throughout our professional lives and the answer to that question may not be particularly good.

Barry-Wehmiller faces the issue head on, publicly stating and then following through with the idea that *"We measure success by how we touch the lives of people"*. The widely known Toyota principle of *'Respect for People'* is actually a rather pithy translation according to Jon Miller. A closer Americanization would be, *"Holding Precious What it is to be Human."* The men and women who work for those companies don't have to worry so much about how they will be eulogized. They get to spend their work week adding to people's lives and no rationalizations or end-of-the-week unsettled feelings are a part of their routines.

There is no reason why every manager cannot feel the same sense of fulfillment as the ones who work for these extraordinary companies, no reason why everyone can't glide seamlessly from the principles they aspire to live up to on

Sunday into the decisions they make at work on Monday. But while committing to those faith driven principles is a necessary start, there is more to it than that. As was mentioned, merely believing is not enough.

While every truly successful company is driven by people of such principles, every person of principle does not necessarily lead a profitable company. That requires a different way of managing – not just a different way of believing. That different way of managing is not just a little different – it is radically different. The way decisions are made at Toyota, ATC, Wahl and the others is very different from conventional companies. Their approach to accounting and how they measure performance is different and often times even their basic organizational structures are different.

These companies understand lean manufacturing at a much higher level than most. They understand that it demands different management processes along with different tools and techniques on the factory floors, but it also centers on a core culture. All three elements are critical: A holistic and humanistic culture, lean management processes, and a battery of execution tools. Without any of the three the success of Barry-Wehmiller or Wahl Clipper is not possible. There can be no emulating Toyota without the three.

Therein lies the problems of Tyson and so many other companies with compassionate people of deep faith at the top. Traditional management principles and practices often run counter to their faith and they find themselves in continual conflict and continually struggling between human goodness and profits; while the management principles and practices of lean drive a synergy between goodness and profits.

So there is the good news – the message of hope for managers who want to put a stop to rationalizing, who no longer want to live with the unsettled feeling, and who want their professional lives to be every bit as great a part of their eulogy as their weekend lives.

The path is clear, and the purpose of this book is to light the way for you.

CHAPTER 2: *More than a 'Feel Good' Culture*

Lean manufacturing is perhaps the most widely misunderstood business concept in history. Experts abound, most of them self-proclaimed with expertise based on the exposure they received to it from a rather limited perspective. By and large, however, it is seen as a unique set of tools. It is too often seen as a series of projects and things to be 'implemented'.

The problem lies in a general under-appreciation for culture, and an unquestioning faith in traditional management practices – particularly in the accounting department. The notion that what they learned in business school is not just off, but completely wrong, is beyond the scope of most folks to wrap their minds around and accept. And culture is generally viewed as a morale issue, but not really at the heart of things. Most top managers are of the opinion that a better culture can make people happier and more productive – lower employee turnover – but not a driver for a completely different way of running the business.

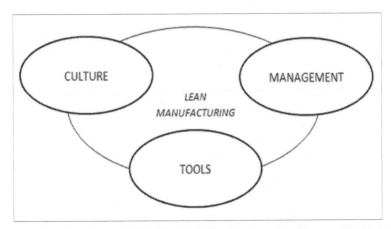

So with culture thus trivialized and management processes assumed to be inherently correct, the understanding of lean is left to the tools. The result is predictable. Lean is written off as a fad, or at best something relevant to factory people but not so much for the rest of the business.

The few companies that go beyond that extremely limited understanding, however, find they have found the key to unlock a door beyond which an amazing business world awaits. In that world the old tradeoffs disappear. Taking very good care of employees, suppliers, customers, and the community doesn't detract from profits – it turbocharges those stakeholders in the business and drives profits to levels previously unimagined.

The heart of lean thinking is the elimination of waste, and waste is defined as anything and everything that does not create value for the end customer. While Bob Chapman finds 'waste elimination' a very uninspiring goal, joking that the only people who can get passionate about eliminating waste are those suffering from severe constipation, Jim Huntzinger would disagree.

Jim is the founder and President of Lean Frontiers, the organization that has probably done more to push the envelope of American understanding of lean thinking and the Toyota System than any other. Jim is also a man of deep faith who shuts down Lean Frontiers every year while he does missionary work in Africa.

Jim looks to the Biblical assertion that God gave man dominion over the earth, and all that is on it; that it was given for man's benefit. It stands to reason that anything we can do to avoid wasting God's gifts is our obligation. A business model centered on consuming only that which enriches the lives of customers and doing our level best to avoid squandering any of God's gifts unnecessarily is a very good thing to do. Jim sees lean not as a career but as an extension of his faith, as a way to work and earn a living while driving to fulfill the highest and best purposes for which we were put on this earth.

But lean is very people centered, as well. When Toyota and the other lean companies give employees an andon cord – the means to literally stop the factory when they see that something is not right – and launch kaizen events – projects in which employees are fully empowered to take matters into their own hands to solve problems and change things for the better – they are living the ideal of servant leadership.

Robert Greenleaf, as the modern day expounder of the servant leadership concept, wrote, *"The difference manifests itself in the care taken by the servant - first to make sure that other people's highest priority needs are being served. The best test, and difficult to administer, is: Do those served grow as persons? Do they, while being served, become healthier, wiser, freer, more autonomous, more likely themselves to become servants? And, what is the effect on the least privileged in society? Will they benefit or at least not be further deprived? "*

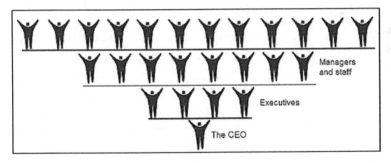

The diagram above represents the idea behind servant leadership. Rather than a top down organization in which everyone's role is to satisfy the person above them, the servant leader is always asking, "How can I help?" Leadership and management exist to enable the folks on the front lines to better serve customers.

The character and values of the servant leader are the same as those of a good parent and contributing member of the community; and those values spring from a belief in a higher power – God – and a conviction that there is something more important than one's self.

The beauty of the people centered approach is that it empowers the people best able to improve things. Not only does flipping the organization upside down and empowering the people on the front lines to call the shots fulfill the best of our faith driven principles – as Bob Chapman said, *"Everybody is somebody's special child"* – it turns out they know more about the details than the most educated manager and can make improvements that dwarf those that management can conjure up.

Eliminating waste and empowering people intersect beautifully. A very influential Japanese industrial engineering pioneer by the name of Yoichi Ueno came to the factory and stop watches by the curious path of a degree in philosophy and a focus on psychology. He viewed time as the most precious of all commodities. Workers and employers both carried a huge moral obligation to respect each other's time. The worker should not steal time from the employer by seeking pay without giving the company their full effort; but likewise the company should never waste an employee's time on work that was not meaningful. Time on this earth is everyone's most precious commodity; the one we can never get back and is so vitally important to be used well.

The resources that are most important to eliminate wasting are people's time and talents. To treat an employee only as a set of hands or a strong back and ignore the fact that he or she is a whole person with a mind and a soul, filled with ideas and aspirations is a waste of money – and more importantly it is a waste of God's creation.

The problems with fully grasping these core lean concepts are daunting. For one (and probably most insurmountable for many) is accounting. Traditional accounting has it backwards. It classifies inventory as an asset, while lean thinking treats it as a squandering – a waste of time and material; a waste of a lot of money. At the same time accounting treats people as expenses that detract from profits. The conventional approach would have us thinking that the key to profitability is to spend less money on our very special human resources, and put it into the wasted resource of inventory instead.

Lean companies focus more on real money instead of accounting and, as we shall discuss in more detail, the two are not the same. And lean companies place more value on common sense than they do on numbers derived by sophisticated formulas and equations. They know what is right and wrong for the long term welfare of the business and all who are a part of it, and that sense of right and wrong trumps accounting every time. As one Canadian manufacturing company President, described it, *"We have to look at the business through our own eyes, rather than through the distorted lens of accounting."*

The traditional company breaks the business down into very small bits and pieces and quite often pits those tiny parts against each other. People are assigned to divisions and departments – "silos" in business parlance. Then hierarchical totem poles are established within the silos. Everyone knows their place and everyone is tasked with optimizing their defined, limited role. How they pursue that optimization and whether it supports or undermines anyone else's optimization efforts is not part of the measurement of a person's performance. Personalities and mastery of internal politics often have more to do with who gets promoted and who gets paid more than anything else.

Lean companies blow up all of those walls and barriers. With scant regard for organizational charts they focus on the overall processes – the series of steps it takes to take an order and turn it into a well satisfied customer. Who does the work, whose idea prevails as the one that best serves the customer, and where the money is spent to best create the value a customer seeks is not important. What is important is that all of the folks along that process work together in the best interest of the customer. Performance is measured through the eyes of customers, rather than through the microscope of cost accounting.

The real confusion regarding lean comes from the apparent contradiction between eliminating waste and fully empowering and supporting people. On the surface, eliminating waste sounds like cost cutting; but how can costs be cut while we pledge to keep good people employed for as long as they will have us as their employer? Where are the savings?

The answer is that lean is not a cost cutting business model at all, despite the best efforts of many, many companies to use the tools of Toyota to do so. In fact, lean is a high octane growth model. The lean machine has no reverse gear, it only goes forward. The objective of that waste elimination is very simple: To free up additional capacity without having to pay for it. When we can stop squandering resources – particularly people's time and talents – on things that customers won't pay for we can apply more of them to things they will pay for. The idea is to create better products – ones that are more valuable to customers – and be able to command higher prices; or to create more of the same products without having to commensurately hire more people and buy more machines to do so.

These differences have broad implications. When we commit to people, doing our best to provide them with a job for life, we have transformed payroll into a fixed cost. When labor becomes a fixed cost standard costing, overhead allocations, unit margin analysis and most of what we do in pricing just got turned on its ear. We have to use a completely different approach to understanding costs and knowing what to charge customers. Taking that completely different approach to accounting is vital, however. We can't hope to treat people with respect and kindness but make decisions based on accounting numbers that treat them as variable costs and little more than expendable tools.

This is the Tyson Chicken dilemma; it is why faith driven leaders still fail or make decisions that may win great favor on Wall Street, but probably raise God's eyebrow.

Just as radical – more so in most companies – when the goal is to sell capacity that has been freed up through employee driven improvement efforts is that the sales folks have to be fully on board and tied at the hip to the effort. Selling capacity, rather than units, requires a collaboration between production, sales and accounting that is often light years away from the typical company environment. In most cases, those functions are isolated from each other; and that is the best case. All too often their relationship is downright adversarial.

These sizeable gaps between traditional management and the lean approach are obstacles to the faith driven leader's success. The right thing to do – the decision that sits best with our conscience and our gut – runs smack into accounting, conflicting departmental goals, and the intramural competition for the next raise or the next promotion, known in most companies as 'politics'. Committing to people and their security and sharing the prosperity of their efforts is exactly the wrong thing to do if viewed through the lens of traditional accounting, where profits are the goal. Reducing inventory in order to free up those resources to create greater customer value actually moves money from the asset column to the expense column according to the accountants. And spending an extra dollar in one part of the organization in order to save two dollars elsewhere is like pulling teeth when the owner of the budget spending the two dollars sees only a negative impact on his performance review.

This is where even the faith driven leader sees principles and profits as trade-offs, rather than as synergistic. This is why it is such a struggle to instill and sustain a principled culture. All of the management forces of the business are pulling away from people and customer centered principles. And this is why the folks working in the middle of this maze of departments and authority levels feel so powerless to work according to their highest values and deepest beliefs.

The Biblical admonition that *"Faith without work is dead"* may well have a business corollary, faith without supportive management processes is equally dead. The good news is that the path is well paved. The likes of Barry-Wehmiller, ATC and others have fully developed and applied the management processes that enable them to turn their commitments to their faith into extraordinary business results.

Matthew wrote, *"To whom much was given, of him much will be required"*. This embodies the spirit of these leaders. They have a deep sense of obligation to the stakeholders of their businesses, viewing their position as a calling instead of an entitlement. Through their refined application of lean management processes, they know just how to meet the requirements they feel God asks of them.

CHAPTER 3: *Stewardship*

Stewardship: the careful and responsible management of something entrusted to one's care.

The intersection of lean manufacturing and faith lies in a strong sense of stewardship. To be sure, the word 'stewardship' is one you hear over and over when talking to successful lean leaders. Without a sense of stewardship business leaders can easily come to see resources – especially human resources – as simply inanimate objects to be leveraged for financial gain. There is no feeling of responsibility for whether those resources were used wisely – just profitably, and the two are not necessarily the same.

The power of lean is that it is an economic model that provides managers with the logic and tools to do both: make a substantial profit through wise stewardship.

Whether a resource is viewed as something God has created, one of our many blessings, or whether that resource is viewed as simply something of value acquired by the business, the objective is the same: To use it wisely and not to squander it. Where lean thinking and traditional management part ways is in that word 'value'. Traditional management sees human beings as little more than unique tools, while lean thinkers see people as the very heart and soul of the organization's reason for existence.

When you consider how companies typically evaluate a potential investment in new machines the value of people becomes starkly apparent. The basic calculation is the cost of performing the work manually is $X while the cost of doing it with automation is $Y. If $X > $Y then the machine is purchased and the person doing the job is eliminated. Reducing human beings to unit costs is the epitome of dehumanization.

From a principled point of view this practice shamefully ignores the fact that the person is so much more than a machine or a tool. It ignores the fact that this is a real thinking, feeling person, loved by someone and put here to fulfill a higher purpose. It ignores the value of that person from a business standpoint as well. It ignores the ability of the person to think, to improvise, and to generate ideas that can make things better for the company and for the customer.

But probably most important is that basic cost math ignores the fact that the person can and should grow and learn over time. The value of the person to the business, given adequate leadership and opportunities, will grow with experience, knowledge, and the wisdom that comes with aging. The machine, on the other hand, will begin to depreciate from the moment it is put on the factory floor.

It is for these reasons that Toyota spurns automation, opting instead for what it calls 'autonomation'. To the casual observer there might not look like there is much difference between a Toyota assembly factory and that of a traditional competitor. Lots of robots can be seen in both factories. But there is a difference and it is the difference (to steal a phrase from Mark Twain) between lightning and lightning bugs. Traditional companies invest in robots to replace human workers. Toyota's autonomation concept is to use robots and other automation to enhance and extend the capability of people.

Toyota wants to keep and take full advantage of the best features of people: their minds principally, but also their innate desire to do good work and to contribute to something worthwhile. Machines can supplement them by doing the work that is dangerous or requires a degree of precision beyond that easily attained by human eyes and hands. Through this combination of people and machines the machines can do what they do best – the heavy lifting so to speak – while people can do what they do best – think.

In a lean company letting a thinking, feeling, growing person go – laying them off – is a shameful waste of a resource that is both precious and has enormous economic value. It is a complete failure of stewardship. The lean manager realizes that hiring is not merely an activity to fill an empty chair on an assembly line, or putting a warm body in front of a machine. It's a promise. The person being hired is making an act of faith – that management knows what it is doing and is providing the means by which the employee can support his or her family. The employee doesn't get to sit in on the meetings at which decisions are made and the strength and vitality of the company are determined. Management does that and the employee is putting their family's security in the hands of management and trusting that those decisions will be made wisely.

Bob Chapman talks a lot about leadership of the business being akin to being the head of the family. He does not mean that in any condescending, paternalistic sort of way, implying that employees are like children. In fact, he sees them as quite the opposite – every bit his equal in the eyes of God. What he means is that, like your children, they are completely at your mercy. The quality of their life is entirely in your hands. A wise parent is self-sacrificing, makes every decision for the good of everyone in the family, balances short term desires with long term goals, and acts with equal love and compassion for each member of the family. That describes lean management as well.

Management stewardship encompasses physical resources beyond people as well. Scrapping poorly made parts or products, using ten pounds of material to make something when it is possible to make it with nine and a half, or consuming more paper or electricity than is absolutely necessary to get the products made are all waste and represent poor stewardship over the assets of the business, as well as equally poor stewardship over God's gifts.

What does Judaism have to say about waste?
"This is the way of the righteous and those who improve society, who love peace and rejoice in the good in people and bring them close to Torah: that nothing, not even a grain of mustard, should be lost to the world, that they should regret any loss or destruction that they see, and if possible they will prevent any destruction that they can."

Jim Huntzinger quotes James Robison and Jay Richards' *"Indivisible: Restoring Faith, Family, and Freedom Before It's too Late"* when he writes: *"'We are responsible for how we treat the earth. Dominion doesn't mean destruction. Since all the earth is God's creation, it has value on its own, apart from what we do with it.' So, therefore, we must work and maintain a strong relationship with Him to understand our role, as deemed by Him, over our tiny part of His creation. We are stewards of part of His creation."*

It doesn't matter what the accountants have to say or where one stands on environmental politics and issues. Wasting resources is poor stewardship no matter one's faith. The core lean principle of eliminating waste can be accurately restated as, 'God gave man dominion over the earth – don't blow it'.

In fact, every faith takes a strong, clear stand on the subject of stewardship with regard to resources. Eliminating waste not only makes good economic sense, it keeps one in good stead with God no matter how one sees or defines God.

It may seem logical to ask 'aren't all businesses, lean or not, interested in eliminating such waste, an effective stewardship of human and physical resources?' In fact, the answer is no. Traditional management accepts a precept that many things are simply necessary – the costs of doing business. Activities such as accounting, administration, scheduling, human resources and the like are viewed as not only necessary but somehow valuable. Lean thinkers see them as wasteful for the simple reason that the people performing these functions and activities are not creating things of value for customers. They are only necessary because of the basic business model decisions the leadership of the company has made. Because they waste people's time, energy and talent on tasks that are not actually benefiting the customers of the business those basic business model decisions and assumptions should be constantly challenged. The goal is to continually devote more and more of the human resources of the company on value creating.

From a spiritual standpoint there is glory and honor in

> If you own a satellite dish odds are it came from the Winegard Company in Burlington, Iowa. Very little of the content comes from offshore. Most of the bits and pieces come from suppliers within a few hours of their plant. They pay higher prices for the parts, but those parts are delivered by twice weekly 'milk runs' in which a truck runs a loop stopping for small quantities from each supplier. The result is radically lower transportation and fuel costs – less waste – and little inventory and its associated costs; all of which more than offset the premium prices for any individual part they buy.

making things – using ones time and talent to transform God's gifts to us into things that make people's lives better. There is not much glory and honor in sitting in front of computer or sifting through stacks of paper. Management has a fundamental responsibility to provide people with meaningful work. This is not to say that everyone who works in management or in an office is performing meaningless work, but that the lean thinker constantly strives to be sure that if those people are not actually making things then all of their efforts are going to support and enhance the efforts of the folks who are, rather than simply performing tasks that have little purpose.

In a similar fashion, traditional companies do look for ways to eliminate wasted materials, energy and the like. However they tend to do so when they can find big heaps of it and to try to eliminate it through grand management and engineering projects and schemes. Lean companies go after it with a singular focus and passion, tasking everyone in the company with finding and eliminating it every day wherever it can be found.

More ominous is that traditional companies manage through accounting systems that do a very poor job of identifying waste. If it isn't visible through accounting it cannot be seen at all in the eyes of traditional managers, or at least it is not viewed as significant. As a result, they tend to focus their cost reduction efforts not on waste but on the very things that are creating value. They ignore all of the waste and instead continually look to eliminate the labor that actually goes into making things, and to reduce the value and cost of the resources that actually go into products.

Rather than effectively steward the human and material abundances with which we have been blessed they quite often misuse the resources that are actually being deployed wisely and pay scant attention to the ones that are being wasted.

In the end, lean is a stewardship model. It is all about accepting both economic and moral responsibility for the time and talent of people, and the materials acquired by the business. And the intersection of faith and lean thinking is clearer nowhere more than in the fierceness with which lean leaders seek and root out any misuse of those resource.

CHAPTER 4: *We're All in This Together*

In September 2014 Congressman Paul Ryan gave a talk titled "The Dignity of Work" to the Torch of Light dinner held by Hebrew University in which he got right to the heart of the intersection of faith and lean manufacturing principles (quite unintentionally I'm sure as I imagine Congressman Ryan knows next to nothing about manufacturing in general let alone lean manufacturing!)

The Congressman said, *"In Catholic social teaching, there are two key principles to keep in mind: solidarity and subsidiarity. Solidarity is a shared commitment to the common good. It's the belief that we're all in this together, and we don't let anybody slip through the cracks. Subsidiarity, meanwhile, is a prudent deference to the people closest to the problem."* Those principles of community and the value of individual people is not just a Catholic teaching but common to all faiths, and common to the thinking of good people who align themselves with no particular faith.

The manner in which most companies are managed, and most business schools teach folks to manage, is the polar opposite of the principles of solidarity and subsidiary.

Traditional management is both siloed and hierarchical. This means, people are divided and largely isolated from each other by function. All of the engineers are in one department, for instance, while all of the purchasing people are in another. Even within production people are further separated, with people who do machining in one area while people who perform assembly work are somewhere else. By hierarchical I mean that within these functional silos there is a pecking order:

The assembler reports upward to an assembly foreman or lead, who, in turn, reports upward to an assembly manager, and so forth.

This approach creates two huge problems in most companies: One, it divides people and sets them in pursuit of departmental or individual goals instead of unifying them in a team with a common goal, namely the fulfillment of customer needs and desires. After all, to satisfy the customer it usually takes people from all of the areas of technical skills and knowledge. Two, the chain of command (or totem pole as it is more often referred to) sends a strong message that the higher up a person is the more important that person is, and authority and compensation increase as one gets higher up within the silo. The worth of people is seen as a function of how much power and authority they have instead of how much they are actually contributing to serving customers. Of course, as one gets higher up in the department they also get further away from where the actual work of creating things of value for customers is being performed.

In a lean environment the basic building block of the organization is not the department, rather it is the value stream. The value stream is the series of steps it takes, cutting across all of the various areas of knowledge and expertise, to take a customer request or requirement from start to finish. There is scant regard for how much or little of the work (or the credit for contributing to success) is allotted to any one area. What matters is that all of the people involved in that value stream work as a team to create the highest value for the customer with the least expenditure of resources for anything that does not help that customer.

That *"shared commitment to the common good"* Ryan spoke of that resonates with people of all faiths was expressed in lean terms by Taiichi Ohno, the former Toyota production director, as follows: *"All we are doing is looking at the time line, from the moment the customer gives us an order to the point when we collect the cash. And we are reducing that time line by removing the non-value added wastes."* Note that there is no mention of the individual, the function or the department. Rather, it is the work done across the time line of working to serve customers that is the focus of the business.

The greatest gulf between our core sense of right and wrong, between the things we know in our personal convictions to be good and the routines of work life in traditional organizations, lies squarely in this difference in focus. As good people – people of faith and service - we want to help and teach other folks. We want to know that we have contributed to other people's growth and development, and that we have used the knowledge and wisdom God has given us for the benefit of the people around us, but the chain of command within siloed organizations creates a strong incentive to do just the opposite

Success in traditional organizations lies not in helping others but in besting them, or often in manipulating them. The way to the top – to greater levels of authority and compensation – is to demonstrate individual superiority. It lies in proving to the boss that you are better than your co-workers, and that you are far superior in knowledge, judgment and work ethic than the lowly people on the front lines.

Instead of helping the people around you become better at what they do; instead of sharing your knowledge and talent with them, there is a powerful incentive to hoard that information and knowledge. You get ahead by simultaneously making them look worse and yourself look better.

The functional structure has very much the same effect. Quite often the way to take better care of the customer, and to make the company more profitable, is to spend an extra dollar in one department in order to save two dollars elsewhere along the path from customer order to delivery. When the ticket to success, however, is to make the boss look good, to enable the department to come in under budget, to demonstrate higher individual efficiency, then there is no incentive to spend that extra dollar. In fact, the incentive is the opposite – to try to compel people from another department to sub-optimize in order to make you and your department look better.

This 'every man for himself', or survival of the fittest culture that defines the keys to career success in most companies contributes more to that sense of disconnection between work and personal values than anything else. In such a culture the person who believes in love for his fellow man and wants to put that conviction into practice is most apt to be trampled by others strongly incented by the opposite principle – the basis for the old saying that nice guys finish last. So there is the moral conundrum so many folks face: How to be a good person, the person you are in your heart but also to be a good provider and to create the quality of life for your family? When your conscience says serve others, while your income grows by looking out for number one?

In a lean environment that conundrum disappears. Success is defined by how the team performs along the entire end-to-end value stream. It is not about how any one person does but how all of the folks with their various and unique skills and knowledge work together and collectively to better serve the customer in the least wasteful manner. Rather than pit people against each other for individual recognition, lean incentivizes people to help each other, and to do whatever they can to make the other folks on the team more capable, to enable them to bring more of their talents to bear on the job. In other words, it drives people to be better practitioners of their faith, rather than worse ones.

When people can come to work on Monday looking forward to practicing that which they professed to believe on Sunday (or Saturday in the case of our Jewish friends), rather than dreading another week of office politics and competing with their co-workers, it makes all the difference in the world. It enables people to believe they are devoting their careers not only to taking better care of their families but taking better care of their souls, as well.

Success in a lean organization in which people are urged to support and complement each other within the value stream drives people to truly appreciate the fact that everyone knows something about the work to be done to go from customer order to customer satisfaction – but no one knows everything. Success demands respecting the role and the knowledge of the other people along that timeline that Ohno talked about, regardless of where they may stand in some departmental totem pole.

Ryan's second point – "*Subsidiarity, meanwhile, is a prudent deference to the people closest to the problem*" – is closely aligned with the first one and also gets at the core of a basic lean principle. That principle is the centrality of the 'gemba'.

Gemba is a Japanese term that means something like 'the site' or the 'real place'. It means the physical location where work is really being done. In lean organizations one hears about 'gemba walks' and 'gemba boards'. A gemba walk is a routine in which senior management people regularly visit the factory floor to engage with the front line production folks in order to better understand the reality of the work, and to learn how they can better support the people who actually create value for customers. Gemba boards are means of tracking how things are going in the actual production areas, typically manually tracked bits of information about the most important things – defects, production levels, and so forth. In a lean environment such gemba boards are more important indicators of how the business is doing than sophisticated computer applications and reports.

The concept of the gemba and the idea that the most important places and people in the company are on the factory floor where people are doing real hands-on work is perfectly aligned with the words of Pope Francis when he said, "*We do not get dignity from power or money or culture. We get dignity from work. Work is fundamental to the dignity of the person. Work, to use an image, 'anoints' with dignity, fills us with dignity, makes us similar to God who has worked and still works, who always acts.*"   When managers go to the gemba they are demonstrating their respect for the work being done there, and for the people who are doing it.

The most powerful aspect of the gemba centered philosophy inherent in lean thinking is that it is the practical application of servant leadership. From Jesus to Muhammad to the Buddha, spiritual leaders have always been servant leaders. They led through their devotion to the success and well-being of others. They acted with humility and put the needs and concerns of others above their own.

The Muslim writer Aisha Stacey said, "*No one who behaves arrogantly or who acts as if he or she has power over others is capable of true submission. All power and strength is from God Alone. All human beings are equal in the sight of God*". That should resonate with everyone of faith. It is hardly a uniquely Muslim tenet.

Lean's gemba focus is the opposite of arrogance, and servant leadership is putting Stacey's words into action. It is said that humility leads to empathy. And in lean cultures that see the work being done in the trenches as the only real value adding work, while everything is waste that can only be justified when

45

it supports the front line folks and enables them to be more successful, empathy for those value adding people is the essential starting place.

The Cherokee have a proverb about two wolves fighting a battle within each of us. The first wolf is the wolf of ego and selfishness. The second is one of humility and empathy; and Cherokee children are taught that the wolf you feed is the one that will win this internal fight and define who you are. Traditional companies drive people to assure the first wolf is well fed, while companies with a strong lean culture offer up a never-ending feast for that second wolf.

In the twin focus on the value stream, rather than the department, and the gemba, rather than the board room, lean companies don't just gain enormous business success through superior customer value creation. They drive people to listen closely to the better angels of their nature.

CHAPTER 5: *It's All About Growth*

To understand how the synergy between lean thinking and the principles that are at the core of good people creates incredible economic success – how lean belies the conventional wisdom that making faith-driven decisions necessarily comes at the expense of lower profits – you have to grasp the fact that lean manufacturing is a lousy cost reduction tool. There is a widespread misconception that lean is a strategy for reducing costs by eliminating waste. Quite to the contrary, lean is an engine for growth.

The purpose of waste reduction and ideally elimination is to free up capacity. And, of course, it has to be this way.

The apparent conflict with lean is the Catch-22 of eliminating waste – unnecessary work - while promising job security to the folks doing that work. How can there be any savings from eliminating unnecessary work if we are going to keep the people doing that work on the payroll and we are going to continue writing the same paychecks to them every week? The answer lies in the economics of Henry Ford.

The roots of lean are very much in the work Henry Ford did in the 1910's and 20's. There are well documented visits by the pioneers of the Toyoda family to Ford's factories in Detroit and Ford's *Today and Tomorrow* is recognized as the original explanation of the waste reduction focus of manufacturing. Toyota Production System originators, Ohno and Shingo, referenced Ford often in their writing with Ohno acknowledging that they learned much of what they know from Ford, asserting, *"If Ford were alive today he would be doing exactly what we are doing"*.

Henry Ford's economic theory was very simple: If it cost $250,000 a day to open up and operate the plant at Highland Park, and the plant produced 1,000 cars, then the cost per car was $250. If they only made 900 cars then the cost was higher - $250,000 ÷ 900 = $278 per car.

He saw just about every cost other than purchased material that went into the car as a fixed cost. All of the people were going to show up for work and all of the lights and machines would be turned on. The cost of all of that was pretty well set. All that mattered – all that could really be controlled – was how many cars flowed across those fixed costs and out the door.

This thinking was the economic impetus for the assembly line, and it is the crux of the economics of the Toyota Production System and lean manufacturing. For that matter it is the key driver of Six Sigma and the Theory of Constraints. Virtually every significant enhancement of manufacturing management theory has had increasing the rate of flow at its core, rather than cost cutting. Getting more output from the existing capacity is the ticket – not reducing headcount.

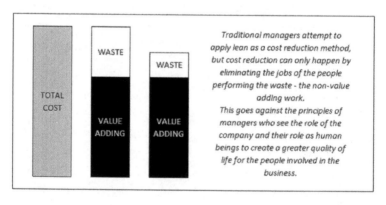

Traditional managers attempt to apply lean as a cost reduction method, but cost reduction can only happen by eliminating the jobs of the people performing the waste - the non-value adding work.
This goes against the principles of managers who see the role of the company and their role as human beings to create a greater quality of life for the people involved in the business.

This is awfully hard to see in traditionally managed companies where reducing the cost of individual items is viewed as a perfectly viable means of increasing profits.

For lean thinkers that idea is a non-starter. For one thing, racing China, Bangladesh or Vietnam to the bottom is a lousy idea. You can't win that race. More important, you can't fulfill the higher purpose lean leaders strive to fulfill by putting less money into the pockets of the stakeholders of the business – the employees, the suppliers, the local community. What is the reason for having the business in the first place, they ask, if it deteriorates the quality of life for most of the people involved in it? Finally, they know that there is a lot more money to be made by the owners of the business through growth than through downsizing, reducing headcount and outsourcing.

To continue the Henry Ford analogy, if Ford could figure out how to have all of those same people come to work, but have the ones doing wasteful, non-value adding work reassigned to work that customers will pay for – work that actually makes the cars better or enables the plant to make more cars – then the math improves.

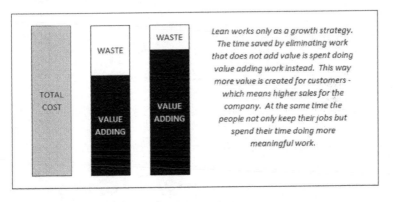

Lean works only as a growth strategy. The time saved by eliminating work that does not add value is spent doing value adding work instead. This way more value is created for customers - which means higher sales for the company. At the same time the people not only keep their jobs but spend their time doing more meaningful work.

We said earlier that if it cost $250,000 per day to run the plant and the plant made 1,000 cars the cost per car was $250. If for the same $250,000 the plant can make 1,100 cars then the cost per car would be $227. This is cost reduction through growth and it is how lean companies eliminate waste while fulfilling their higher mission of improving the quality of people's lives.

It should come as no surprise that a number of the companies mentioned so far have expansion projects planned to accommodate their growth. Aluminum Trailer and Wahl Clipper have major construction projects underway. Lynne Henson, president of Superior Abrasives in Ohio says, *"Superior has been growing rapidly in recent years,"* and she has launched a new factory construction project. And that she *"Personally trained all my managers in lean to make sure they weren't defeating what I was trying to implement and so that the people on the shop floor were in good hands."* It comes as no surprise that, when asked about her interests outside of running the company, she also says, *"I love helping through our church, so I would be out doing some kind of ministering in one regard or another."*

The nexus of lean thinking, belief in a higher purpose and business success through growth, is clear. Principled lean leaders want more profits, not for the sake of more profits, but because more profits mean more employees making more money, more money into the community, more customers benefiting from the products, more good suppliers taking care of more people as a result of the partnership, and, of course, more for the stockholders.

Traditional leaders want more profits too, but lean leaders outperform them because the traditional managers want more profit for their own sake and that of the owners. The rest of the stakeholders are often their adversaries – folks whose jobs, paychecks and contracts are targets for cutting in pursuit of those profits. Hardly a formula for enlisting their support in the profit maximization effort.

From a practical standpoint, converting non-value adding jobs to value adding is difficult. More often than not the way it happens is that the people doing the wasteful work are simply able to support higher volumes. For instance, if the company needs to inspect 100% of their products before shipping in order to assure quality, when they eliminate defects through lean tools such a polka yoke – mistake proofing a process to a point that defects are impossible to create - it may be possible to only inspect half of the products, thus enabling the same number of inspectors to support twice as much production. As a result the non-value adding cost of quality inspection is only half as much.

This is the capacity expansion goal of lean at work. Ideally the fixed cost base is reduced, but it is just as effective if the fixed costs can be maintained while a higher volume flows across them.

Accounting, again, is the culprit that makes this simple approach to economic success so hard to see. It is what leads even faith driven leaders like those at Tyson to shatter people's lives through layoffs and plant closings under the belief that such actions are their only course in order to "cut expenditures" and "improve efficiencies"; which they believe are necessary in order to improve profits.

In fact, no company has ever cut its way to success, whether it defines success in purely financial terms or as it properly should - in terms of its human impact; in Bob Chapman's terms – by how it affects the lives of people. Success can only come from more, and you can't cut your way to more.

CHAPTER 6: *Hard Core Culture*

Lean is really a holistic approach to business, this is the true root of the widespread misunderstanding of lean.

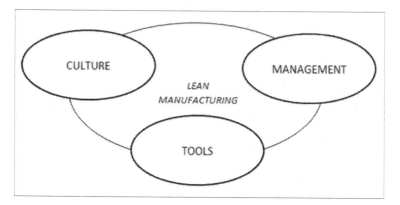

In most companies that think they are pursuing lean they are actually only deploying a set of lean tools – kanban or demand pull, SMED or set-up time reduction, U-Shaped production cells and so forth. Management processes are seen as outside of the scope of lean. And culture, if it is addressed at all is either a kumbaya sort of 'feel good' idea, or a paternalistic approach that's centered around throwing bones to employees in the form of extra fringe benefits or company paid pizza parties.

In fact, at a recent lean management event I stepped out of an elevator at the Drake Hotel in Chicago and ran into John Cook, the owner and CEO of yet another extraordinarily successful, very lean company, Stainless Design, in Hamilton New Zealand. When I asked John how the event was going for him he replied that he *"was struck by how nice everyone was. All of the participants were genuinely good people, kind and more than willing to share."* That conversation was the spark that led to starting to write this book the next week.

Of course the folks there were nice. I don't know of anyone who is successful in the lean world who is not nice. But their niceness isn't the key to their success. It is the underlying driver of niceness that also drives their success.

Now there is absolutely nothing wrong with being nicer to the folks we work with, and just about everyone is glad to have a free slice of pepperoni, but that is not what lean culture is all about. At its heart, lean culture is about respect – not phony, lip service respect but genuine respect.

And it involves very specific behaviors and means of communicating and solving problems. There are rules to be followed, and consequences for failure to follow them!

Unlike most human endeavors lean culture is not a blame culture. When something goes wrong, while most managers want to know who screwed up or who is responsible for the problem; in a lean organization the assumption is that the cause of the problem is almost always a poorly designed process, it is no one's fault. We could get rid of the person at the point of the problem and replace him with just about anyone and the same problem would eventually resurface because that person would be attempting to execute a flawed process.

No, in a lean culture the person at the point of the failure is thanked for bringing the problem to light. The organization cannot get better unless people willingly point out failures. Only then can we fix the underlying process and execute better in the future.

The traditional culture of blame, and its companion - arrogance - are a disease that causes most companies to fail from the inside out. Managers sit around and blame hourly folks' laziness and attitude for the problems; the people on the shop floor blame lousy management; and they all agree that their biggest problems are caused by the government and its excessive tax burden and regulations. The common theme is that our lack of success is always someone else's fault, and that someone else is almost always someone who isn't in the room.

This constant seeking of someone to blame is what fuels a 'kill the messenger' culture, in which admitting to a mistake or a problem for which one needs help solving can be tantamount to career suicide. It actually rewards people whose contribution is little more than effectively finding and highlighting other's mistakes.

Such a culture, if nothing else, proves the Biblical adage about seeing the splinter in the other fellow's eye with much greater clarity than seeing the log in one's own eye. And it flies directly into the face of Jesus' suggestion that only the sinless are qualified to cast stones.

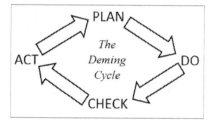

Lean culture – celebrating facts and bringing problems to light as the best and really only way to improve feels a whole lot better for those involved. This open and honest culture is seen in another core facet of the lean culture; and that is the PDCA (Plan-Do-Check-Act) Cycle. This is basically the idea that our solutions, schemes, plans and ideas might be good but they are not likely to be perfect. So when we get together to solve a problem or make a change, we are going to implement it in a small way, then loop back and seek out all of the things that weren't so perfect and fix them, then launch again and loop back again until we are satisfied.

The PDCA idea is directly counter to the culture in which someone brings forth an idea and that person's internal competitors for the next raise or promotion are sitting like vultures waiting to prove its failure. In such a culture, destroying other's ideas is just as likely to lead to a raise in status and money as bringing forth ideas of one's own. Accounting culture, in particular, is quite often based on criticism with no expectation of accountants to ever bring forth operational improvement strategies of their own creation.

The core concept of respect for people is not just theoretical or philosophical respect based on the belief that we are all children of God and equal in His eyes. It is professional respect, as well. It is based on the knowledge that no one knows everything about a process or an operation, but everyone involved knows something. It is only when we get all of the folks involved with all of that collective knowledge together, regardless of title or paycheck, and pool the collective thinking that we can truly understand the issue and come up with truly effective solutions.

This is probably the best place in the book to bring up the truest alignment between lean and faith – the quest for unattainable perfection. People of faith universally accept the idea that none of us are perfect; we are all flawed, but our quest in life is to become better people, better servants of God, and better examples of His teachings every day. In other words, we are all on a journey of continuous improvement. In Japanese, and in universal lean jargon, kaizen is exactly that – continuous improvement.

If one were to visit Toyota and ask what their approach to business is all about they would probably bring out this rather boilerplate diagram:

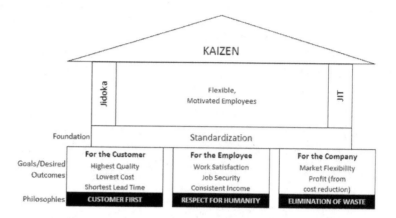

As the chart shows, all of the underpinnings are directed at kaizen – continuous improvement - the never ending quest for perfection; getting better every day. Lean companies don't measure themselves against their competition, budgets or prior years. Such metrics lead to complacency and an overly conservative approach – 'Things are going pretty good – better not change anything and risk screwing it up'. Instead, they measure themselves against perfection, and create a sense of urgency in the realization that they always have a long way to go. Where traditional companies are reluctant to change, with management processes that stifle creativity and innovation, kill ideas at the source and maintain the status quo; lean companies see everything as up for grabs and ripe for improvement all the time. Nothing is perfect so nothing is exempt from improvement ideas.

In their outstanding book, *Creating a Kaizen Culture*, Jon Miller and Mike Wroblewski included the following:

"We say that an organization has a kaizen culture when...

✓ *it values and develops people;*

✓ *builds trust through shared purpose;*

✓ works toward the long-term interest of all stakeholders;

✓ imagines and communicates a positive vision for the future;

✓ creates an environment in which the exposure of problems, abnormalities, and inconsistencies is not only allowed but encouraged;

✓ treats failures as learning laboratories;

✓ follows a common approach to solving problems scientifically;

✓ makes decision based on data and facts;

✓ holds strong beliefs, assumptions, and values about what is right and good;

✓ maintains a sense of humility to seek out and digest foreign ideas and viewpoints;

✓ takes intelligent risks;

✓ and takes the time to plan thoroughly and build consensus but also acts with a sense of urgency."

These 12 points say quite a bit, and they clearly demonstrate how far beyond kumbaya and pizza the lean culture goes. Note that this is not a twelve item cafeteria of lean culture options and possibilities. Each are essential in their own right, and each interacts with the others. They represent an 'all or none' proposition.

Most, if not all, of them are touched upon in one place or another in this book, but the second one – "builds trust through shared purpose" merits particular emphasis.

In speaking to leadership and management teams my typical spiel goes something like this:

"If an employee were to come up to you and ask what the purpose is, what the goal is, why he and everyone else should knock themselves out to get the job done, how would you answer? Is it to create an ever bigger sack of cash to give to whoever owns the place? If that's the answer then do you really think anyone is going to get out of bed a little earlier, put a little extra hop in their step, stay a little later if it is just to meet that goal?

I hope you don't answer that the employee should do it for the money — that he can get a raise and earn a little more by hopping to it to meet that goal a little better. If so - if you really reduce the whole thing to each person being out for their own financial gain - then every sane employee should leave you the minute they find someone else willing to pay a nickel more an hour than you do.

You better have a much better answer than that one if you expect the folks in your organization to drive you to excellence. You better have a shared purpose that goes well beyond each person's wallet.

A much better answer might be this one: You have 250 employees, and each of them has a spouse or a significant other of some kind, so you really have 500 people depending on the paychecks you cut. But it certainly doesn't stop there. Each of those couples probably has 2 point something dependents — their kids or elderly parents — just about everyone has people depending on them for support. So it is now over a thousand. But that's just the start.

Those paychecks total better than $10 million that you pump into the local economy. How many local pizza places, gas stations and small businesses depend on that $10 million for their survival? And, of course, they have employees, and the owners and employees have spouses and kids. And this doesn't *begin to get into your suppliers who are getting perhaps $20 million or more from you, and all of them have employees with families who depend on your business for their livelihood.*

Do the math and you and 250 people have the quality of life of thousands of people in your hands. You get it right and all of thousands of people – people who have no say in how you do things here but are completely dependent on you to get it right – can live a pretty high quality life. Screw it up and all of those people who put their faith in you are in trouble.

What you are doing here has darn little to do with any of you and your personal desire to get rich. It has everything to do with the heavy mantle of responsibility on your shoulders to come through for all of those spouses, kids, old folks, small business people who have put it in your hands.

My advice to you is to recognize this as your shared purpose, and to recognize that you need everyone – each person in the company – all hands on deck – in order to meet this responsibility. And the best part is that if you do get it right, then you can hire more people, and you can all make more money, and you can touch the quality of life for more people. That is a goal worth getting out of bed a little earlier for."

Once again, the central point is made – when the folks at any company saddle up for a shared purpose that embraces everyone with a stake in the company, accepting particular responsibility for those who have no control over things – they serve God and man. They make profits beyond anything a company driven solely by shareholder value can make, and they devote their time and talent to work that serves their true purpose for being on this earth quite fully.

The task of converting an old culture to a lean culture is not easy, and living and maintaining that culture can be even tougher. Living by one's principles rarely is easy – no reason to think it would be much different at work. But the promise and what makes it worth-while is that it is the key to simultaneous fantastic business success and personal fulfillment for everyone involved.

CHAPTER 7: *Accounting*

Throughout much of this book traditional accounting practices have fallen under heavy criticism. There is good reason for that: It is both incorrect, at least insofar as it does not generate numbers by which to make good business decisions, and it institutionalizes and tends to validate management practices that lead to many of the abusive practices that have been cited throughout the book.

Over the past twenty or thirty years there has been a growing trend of managing by the numbers, rather than by wisdom, judgment and good business sense. Not only has this led to treating people as mere figures on a spreadsheet, it has led to very poor business decisions, especially in the manufacturing arena. Accounting has moved from a support function (paying the bills and keeping track of things) to a central role in strategic decision making. In many companies the path to leadership goes through the financial function, rather than from career paths that demonstrate solid mastery of the products and how they are made.

Several years ago I was walking through the factory of an aluminum extruder in Minnesota, a company that was almost tunnel visioned on direct labor costs to the exclusion of just about everything else, even though direct labor costs were only about 8-9% of their total costs. I asked the manufacturing manager who was giving me the plant tour why he thought management was so preoccupied with the cost of people actually making things – actually creating value for customers.

His answer: *"Because it is easy to count."* He was exactly right. A financial statement includes some things that are fairly accurate, and quite a few things that are not; and it completely ignores many important things that we have no way of quantifying and putting into terms of dollars and cents.

The numbers themselves are chock full of allocations, assignments and accruals – all accounting methods to identify costs with activities and time frames that are not real, but represent accounting's best estimate of where they should be. And the statements say nothing at all about the economic impact and value of people's knowledge and experience; the impact of people's ideas and ability to solve problems; the value of a safe, clean workplace or the benefits of cross-training people so they have a broad range of skills.

The net effect of this is that, with management looking only at the numbers that are "easy to count" – largely the cost of people - and no way of knowing the value of those people, making decisions by the numbers often leads to disastrous results for the business and especially for the people. People are reduced to costs, and headcount.

There is a gross misconception that accounting is correct, proven, and infallible and that there is only one way of calculating costs and the numbers on the standard battery of financial statements are the product of that one correct way. Nothing could be further from the truth. Lean companies do the math differently, and as a result make decisions differently.

With the stroke of a pen lean companies change labor costs from variable to fixed – treat labor cost like the cost of rent, a cost that will be the same no matter what management does. That simple decision all but takes people's paychecks off the table for management's decision making, and it changes everything. Product pricing, how to reduce costs and what drives higher profits are all seen differently when labor is treated as a fixed cost.

That is but one of a number of differences between how accounting is traditionally performed and how lean companies keep their books, but for the manager driven by higher principles it goes a long way toward eliminating the moral conflicts between work life and personal values. People are no longer treated as a financial drag on profits, but as an asset, and like every other asset, people should be well taken care of and fully utilized.

Before we get too far, it is important to point out that accounting has two facets: Financial Accounting, which is the generation of numbers and reports for entities outside of the company … entities such as investors, bankers and stock brokers. Those numbers, as a matter of law, must be created according to GAAP – Generally Accepted Accounting Principles.

The other side of accounting is Management Accounting, or Managerial Accounting. This encompasses all of the reports and numbers used for internal management decision making … things such as budgets, product costs, pricing and so forth.

GAAP accounting is a lot like ones income taxes. Whether the numbers are useful or accurate really doesn't matter. They are calculated the way the regulations dictate them to be calculated. The IRS dictates that you will deduct $3,950 for each dependent on your 2014 tax return. Period. Presumably that number has some logic behind it somewhere, but it has nothing to do with the cost or value of any of your dependents. Right, wrong, or indifferent, however, you must use that figure or you will be in hot water with the IRS.

No one with any sense would use that number to make important decisions in their lives. You would be foolish to assume the cost of having another child is $3,950 (or even to adjust your taxes by $1,000 for the standard child tax credit allowance) simply because the IRS has set certain figures in place. It would be absurd to pull out last year's Form 1040 to answer your spouse's question as to whether you can afford to take the kids to Disney World. The tax return serves a particular, narrow purpose, and making practical financial decisions is not that purpose.

Likewise, GAAP accounting serves a very narrow purpose. It is intended to provide outside entities with consistent information about businesses – it is particularly for investors. It would be very difficult for you to decide whether to buy stock in Ford or General Motors if each of those companies did their accounting in entirely different ways. So GAAP lays down the rules to enable an investor to make an apples to apples comparison.

When you look at a GAAP compliant balance sheet it includes some very accurate figures – how much cash the company has in the bank, for example – and some numbers that have little precision at all – like the value of the inventory the company has in the warehouse. GAAP inventory is the product of quite a few rather shaky allocations and assumptions. While the inventory value has little bearing on reality, the redeeming value of GAAP accounting is that both companies calculated it by pretty much the same math. So you don't really know what the real asset value is of either Ford or General Motors but you can get a consistent, general sense of the value of one company in comparison to the other.

That's it. That's all GAAP does, and all it is intended to do. The problem with the accounting profession is that it views GAAP as truth. Perhaps it is because so much time is devoted to it in Accounting school, perhaps because, like all government regulated endeavors it is ridiculously convoluted, or perhaps because it makes accounting life easier; but regardless of the reason, the accounting profession as a whole has insisted on using GAAP numbers to drive the Managerial Accounting side of things. This is where lean and traditional management part ways.

Just the same as you would not use your tax return as the basis for deciding whether to take the family to Disney World or not, lean companies don't use GAAP statements and their derivatives to make business decisions. Just like at home, lean managers use a combination of accounting, cash, and common sense and judgment to manage the business.

The details of how performance is measured and pricing and spending decisions are made in a lean accounting environment is beyond the scope of this book. There are several outstanding sources for such information that treat those subjects very well; Brian Maskell's *Practical Lean Accounting* is perhaps the best and most widely read.

The important aspects of lean accounting, and how they support the decisions a principled, faith driven manager make include:

- Collecting costs and measuring things based on cross functional value streams, rather than in each functional silo. This approach recognizes the teamwork and normal integration needed to achieve excellence. Lean management doesn't want people pitted against each other, or departments battling over supremacy. Rather, it wants people to make decisions for the good of the whole, and especially for the good of the customer. It wants people to willingly spend an extra dollar somewhere in the value stream if by spending that dollar it can save two dollars somewhere else along the chain of activities; or if by doing so the company can create more than a dollar's worth of additional value for customers.

- Lean accounting is based on cash – real money – while traditional accounting deals in 'paper profits' and numbers that do not reflect actual money coming into and out of the business. As a result, lean companies relentlessly drive inventory out of the business, while traditional companies treat inventory as an asset. Lean companies succeed largely because of this. Only under GAAP driven accounting does buying or making things that customers don't need, building a warehouse to hold it in, filling that warehouse with racks and forklifts, paying people to move it around, and using a big computer to track it all make sense. Lean companies, driven by cash, see all of that as the colossal waste of money and profit that it really is. Lean companies view all of the reasons for carrying inventory as thinly veiled excuses for failing to identify and eliminate underlying problems, such as poorly operating machines, excessively long lead times, or taking too long to change machines over from one product to the next.

- Lean accounting largely does away with the various types of cost types typically assigned to them by accounting – fixed versus variable, direct or indirect, overhead, etc.. Virtually all costs are treated as fixed in a lean environment, with the exception of direct materials, and if costs are broken down into categories at all they are separated into value adding and non-value adding.

> *"One might say that American manufacturing cost management practice could be depicted as a cat wildly chasing its tail of 'unit cost'. "*
>
> **H. Thomas Johnson**

- Standard costs are done away with in lean. They are costs used under GAAP to value inventory but lean managers see them as misleading and potentially dangerous numbers, not at all reflective of reality, and used too often to make poor decisions.

In the broadest sense, lean accounting is very little accounting at all. Lean thinking is driven by the concept that costs are fixed, profits are the result of driving production flow increasingly faster across that fixed cost base, and people can create enormous value by making a myriad of small improvements and solving the small problems that impede that flow.

The value adding costs of material and direct labor are where value is created for customers – that which pays for the whole shebang. As a result they are not targets for relentless attack but things to be nourished and enriched. It is all the rest of the costs – problems on the shop floor, excessive management and administration, transportation and packaging, and the cost of massive computer hardware and software, and all the people needed to keep the computers well fed – that are the enemy. These costs do not create value for customers and since customers won't assume the cost of them, they are the appropriate targets for elimination.

Numbers with dollar signs in front of them are often useful, but just as often not; as with numbers without dollar signs. The objective of a lean company is to continually improve the processes from supplier to customer – speed them up by eliminating the waste. Accounting numbers – especially those derived from GAAP – are not very useful in this endeavor. In fact, they serve to sustain the old wasteful processes.

Henry Ford once said that, *"Profit is the inevitable conclusion of work well done."* Lean and lean accounting very much support this principle. Focus on the processes, involve and show deep respect for the people who are actually engaged in the processes, continually drive out the defects, delays, and unnecessary work, and the customers will reward you handsomely. The companies I have cited throughout this book, and many others, are the real examples of just how much wisdom was in Ford's words.

Most important, had they been using lean accounting, rather than GAAP driven accounting, I have no doubt the good folks at Tyson Foods would have seen that whatever financial problem they faced – whatever caused them to think they needed to *"cut expenditures"* and *"improve efficiencies"* – had a much more beneficial and powerful solution than driving good employees out of their company. They could have driven profits up in the same manner Berry-Wehmiller, ATC and the rest do, through their Christian values, rather than having to compromise those values.

Understanding the business through the accounting system cannot help but to dehumanize the business, which flies in the face of everything people of faith and principles believe in. Lean companies bring out the accounting system, overhaul it so that it reflects the way they want to manage the business, then kick it into the background and manage the business directly, relegating accounting to a side issue – numbers that are occasionally helpful but not central to decision making. In doing so they re-humanize the business.

CHAPTER 8: *Don't Look to Academia or Wall Street*

March 25, 1911 was a Saturday. That didn't matter much in the sweatshop days of that era, and it particularly didn't matter at the Triangle Shirtwaist Factory, an operation taking up the top three floors of the ten story Asch Building. (A 'shirtwaist" was the common term at the time for a woman's blouse.) The building is now part of New York University with a lovely view of Washington Square Park in Greenwich Village. Back then it was a quite a bit different and the neighborhood was far from the trendy one it is today.

The factory employed some 600 people, most of them recent immigrant women and teenage girls, very few of whom spoke English, earning $15 a week or so for standard 60 hour work weeks - $3-4 an hour by today's standards. Almost a fourth of those workers didn't come home after work that day as the result of a fire that was the worst industrial incident in American history. 145 workers died in the fire causing a shock to the national senses. The Triangle Shirtwaist Factory fire was a watershed event for American manufacturing.

Three out of four elevators weren't working, the owners had not installed a sprinkler system. Of the two doors to the stairways leading to the street one was locked from the inside to prevent anyone from leaving early. Women died of fire and smoke inhalation, some died having jumped or climbed down the elevator shafts, and in a scene that was an eerie premonition of the of the World Trade Center disaster of 100 years later, 58 girls chose to jump from the tenth floor to certain death rather than be taken by the fire.

It was a horror beyond anything in American industrial history and it set off a series of laws and changes in industrial safety that eventually put an end to sweatshops in the United States.

The aftermath of the Triangle Shirtwaist factory fire reflected our national values. While there will always be a minority of folks who are willing to pursue money with the blatant disregard for human life of Max Blanck and Isaac Harris, the owners of the Triangle Shirtwaist Company and who had a long history of such a depraved approach to management; and there will always be a minority of Americans willing to look the other way and buy goods made by such people, collectively as a nation we decided that basic values trumped company profits and lower cost goods. We decided that, while we are all in when it comes to free enterprise and competition, there had to be limits on bringing about human suffering in the course of it.

Or did we?

A hundred years and a couple of months after the Triangle Shirtwaist factory nightmare, an event of appalling similarity took place. On November 24, 2012 117 women died making clothing, mostly for American women, in a sweatshop fire. The same inadequate fire prevention systems, locked doors, negligent management. The women made even less than those at the Triangle Shirtwaist Factory - $38 a month for similarly long hours and similarly brutal working conditions.

The big difference was that this fire happened in the Tazreen Fashions Factory in the Ashulia District on the northwest side of Dhaka Bangladesh, a sprawling mass of industrial buildings where some 6 million people live in mostly deplorable conditions and work in wretched factories making things – primarily clothing – for westerners.

And the Tazreen Fashions fire paled in comparison to what happened seven months later: Five miles down the road from the Tazreen Fashions Factory the Rana Plaza factory building collapsed killing more than 1,100 people, all of them working in similar conditions for similarly low wages, and the victims of similar management disregard for human life.

It would appear as though we have collectively lowered our values from those we held when the laws and regulations preventing such atrocities from happening were passed following the Triangle Shirtwaist Factory fire. Perhaps, but what has really happened is that we have turned the decision making for what is ethical and what is right over to business. Where American society has precluded such abusive practices within our shores, each company now has its own authority to define what is right and what is wrong. Clearly many have set the bar much lower than Americans have as a whole.

Since NAFTA was enacted some twenty or more years ago there has been a flurry of global trade agreements that typically pay little more than lip service to moral and ethical issues. Companies have had the doors opened to manufacture or contract their manufacturing to places throughout Asia, Central America and elsewhere in which there is far less regard for human life than that which we collectively expressed through laws and regulations regarding everything from child labor, working conditions, basic building and factory safety and environmental impact.

Those same trade agreements have had the effect of causing American environmental regulations to be something of a sham – a sort of 'feel good environmentalism'. With the doors open to manufacture just about anywhere, great swaths of American manufacturing has moved to places such as China and Vietnam where there has been little or no environmental concern. The result is cleaner air and water in the United States but shocking levels of air and water pollution on the other side of the planet. Overall the planet is worse for it, but it enables Americans to feel good for having cleaned up our corner of the world – never mind that we are the consumers of the products being made in those toxic wastelands – the visibility in the Chinese city of Harbin is routinely as low as 50 meters, and 16,000 dead pigs floated down the toxic Huangpu River. China has reached the point of a full blown environmental crisis.

The companies sourcing in the deathtrap factories of Bangladesh are almost all large, publicly traded ones. They do so under enormous pressure from Wall Street for very short term profits, and the leaders of those companies have a couple of very fundamental differences from those of the privately held companies most likely to be reading this book.

In the Introduction I wrote, "*When the company exists with an ending objective of making money then it is bound by no principles – money has no morals. But when making money is the second last step – the final objective is something else – something to be done with the money that is good – the entire company pursues profits within a moral code that changes everything.*" Publicly traded firms, by their very nature, exist only to make money. In spite of the frequent outcry for social responsibility as a matter of corporate law unless there is a clearly delineated corporate charter to the contrary (and even that is subject to change at any board meeting) any other goal is impossible.

In the typical publicly traded company, the relationship of the owners with the company is more like your personal relationship with a Las Vegas casino – that is to say there is no personal relationship at all. The company is purely a potential source of financial gain, and the investor is completely willing to sever the relationship in an instant if he or she believes there is a greater financial advantage to investing their money elsewhere.

Those anonymous investors generally have no particular time frame for their financial relationship other than the driving desire to gain as much money from the relationship as soon as possible. The whole system is rigged with a bias toward the extremely short term, however, and therein lies a huge problem. The brokers and traders who actually buy and sell the stock for the investors are usually compensated via commissions for each trade and therefore have a very strong incentive to keep the stock churning and moving from one company to another frequently.

This is in very sharp contract with the owners of the privately held firm. They tend to be in it for the long term, especially in family owned firms. They worry more about what their children and grandchildren will have than any near term profit figures. They also tend to be cash focused, while the big guys worry about paper profits – I often joke with the owners of smaller firms that their idea of utopia is positive cash flow with a paper loss to avoid having to pay taxes. The public firms seek just the opposite – cash is a commodity and calculated profits are everything. In fact, they go to extraordinary creative lengths to inflate profits, then even greater creative lengths to come up with techniques to minimize taxes on those profits.

The owners of smaller and medium sized companies also tend to be much closer to the communities in which they operate, and to their employees. This is far less apt to be true of the public companies that often invest in communities purely for tax and other financial incentives, and have their plants run by managers brought in from the outside who have no ties to the community, and don't expect to be there long enough to put down roots.

In a larger sense, despite all of the publicity the CEO's of the big publicly traded firms receive, they are really leaderless companies. Consider the following:

Technically a Papal Encyclical is a letter from the Pope to the bishops of the Catholic Church described as intending to *"condemn some prevalent form of error, point out dangers which threaten faith or morals, exhort the faithful to constancy, or prescribe remedies for evils foreseen or already existent."* Popes don't write them too often but the recent practices of the multi-nationals (among other concerns) prompted Pope Benedict to write one a few years ago entitled CARITAS IN VERITATE, or 'Charity in Truth'.

In his encyclical he wrote, *"... there is nevertheless a growing conviction that business management cannot concern itself only with the interests of the proprietors, but must also assume responsibility for all the other stakeholders who contribute to the life of the business: the workers, the clients, the suppliers of various elements of production, the community of reference. In recent years a new cosmopolitan class of managers has emerged, who are often answerable only to the shareholders generally consisting of anonymous funds which de facto determine their remuneration. By contrast, though, many far-sighted managers today are becoming increasingly aware of the profound links between their enterprise and the territory or territories in which it operates."*

That well known CEO is actually *"answerable only to the shareholders generally consisting of anonymous funds."* To be sure, he answers to a board of directors but they answer to fund managers and a huge number of investors who individually amount to nothing. He is answerable, in fact, to Wall Street and its reaction to quarterly earnings reports and short term projection. Unlike the owner of a privately held company there is no one at the top of the publicly traded firm with the authority to make ethical and principle based decisions, especially if those decisions might be perceived to cause profits to be less. He is, for all practical purposes, answerable completely to numbers, rather than to people, and numbers have no moral code. In their book, Creating a Kaizen Culture, Jon Miller and Mike Wroblewski said that an essential aspect of the highly successful company is that it *"holds strong beliefs, assumptions, and values about what is right and good."* In the publicly traded firm, answerable to the *"anonymous funds"* the Pope wrote of, there is enormous pressure to define what is *"right and good"* as just about anything that is legal that increase profits – all in all a pretty low standard. Hence the Tazreen Fashions Factory fire and the environmental disaster in China.

The purpose of this chapter is to draw the distinction between the environment in which the publicly traded firms operate and that of the privately held companies; and to make the point that a principled manager should not look to the publicly traded companies for management leadership. If the truth were known, most of them are not that well managed in the first place. Regardless, they seek to attain different goals, and therefore, have a different view of management.

Unfortunately, the business press and the academic community idolizes – or detests – these big companies and focuses just about all of their attention on them. A few years ago I wrote a blog piece that criticized a paper written by a couple of college professors describing clever ways to manipulate inventories to optimize earnings. I received an email from one of them, a leading professor at Michigan State University, asking for more detail concerning the basis for my criticism. I described lean accounting to her and she was excited at the prospect of learning more about it – until she found out that all of the practitioners are smaller and medium sized privately held firms. If none of the big guys were pursuing lean accounting, she had no interest. And that is typical of the academic community.

The biggest problem with looking to the big companies for management leadership is that they have a very fundamental different idea of value. The principles of lean management and lean accounting are centered on maximizing customer value, while the publicly traded firms focus on maximizing shareholder value. The two may align, but usually not.

In optimizing customer value, lean management views the ratio of money spent on things customers will pay for – good materials, the right features, excellent quality workmanship – as a percentage of total spending as the critical driver of success. The more that is spent on those things, the higher prices and more products will be sold. Money spent on other things is money wasted for the simple reason that customers will not reimburse you for them.

The publicly traded firms actually drive to minimize value adding – focusing on hammering down direct labor and beating suppliers down – and scour the world looking for cheaper sources of those things. Hence the Tazreen and Rana Plaza factory tragedies. They view management as the essential element of business and spend an enormous amount of money on it, including often palatial corporate headquarters, large corporate staffs and extremely sophisticated information management systems. Lean companies see all of those things as waste; they don't create value for customers and are a drain on profits.

Another marked difference is the investment in marketing, advertising and brand management. The old time comedian and social commentator Will Rogers once said, *"If advertisers spent the same amount of money on improving their products as they do on advertising then they wouldn't have to advertise them."* Lean managed companies take this as a matter of common sense. Some amount is necessary in order to introduce customers to the company and its products to start

76

out, but it is the product and service that speak for themselves and define the brand in the long term. And expenses for advertising and marketing cannot be passed onto customers. To do so simply drives up the price relative to the value provided and loses business.

In sharp contract a company such as Campbell (the soup company) is quite typical. With massive investments in advertising, a large corporate headquarters and an enormous ERP system the amount of money they actually spend on the product – making soup – is less than half of their total spending. Compare that with the 60-70% or more that the highly successful lean companies normally spend on the product.

The large, publicly traded companies' business model has evolved to a predictable and typically marginally successful one at best: Strive for innovation – create a steady stream of new products to make up for the fact that customers are less and less willing to buy the old ones. Note that the Campbell situation is typical. People are still buying plenty of chicken noodle soup – just more and more of the private or store label brands because they have learned that it is often a much better value for the price. Then pour huge amounts of money into advertising in order to create a big, immediate stir. The amount of money that goes to ad agencies is often amazing, and the resulting ads more often than not revolve around sex and humor in order to get attention, rather than having much to say or do with the product. Then pay for all of that with a relentless focus on finding ever cheaper labor and ever cheaper materials with which to make the product. Finally they attempt to control the far flung supply chains and the massive inventories needed to support them with outrageously expensive computer systems.

There is nothing particularly unprincipled by the various management techniques the publicly traded firms have developed and honed over the years. It is simply that they are techniques have been developed to achieve goals that are devoid of principles.

All of it serves to generate high short term sales and profits, but once the initial buzz wears off and they need to rely on repeat business, the bottom often falls out, and the cycle repeats. In the short term the spikes can drive stock prices up and make some investors very happy and very wealthy. In the long term, however, the decreasing understanding of and attention to value erodes and ultimately destroys the company. Their histories tend to show them going from spike to spike, with every spike followed by a new CEO and a restructuring plan. Mergers and acquisitions are central to their strategies as they look to buy up small companies with good customer value propositions ... then usually destroy them.

Because the publicly traded firms are focused on and answerable only to Wall Street, GAAP accounting – the set of numbers legally mandated to report to Wall Street – almost always rule the day, and all of the problems resulting from using those numbers that were described in the last chapter are commonplace. Those companies also tend to be led by people whose background is financial, or from the sales and marketing area, since those areas are the heart of their management thinking. This too has a major impact on their inability to create superior value. More important, those functions are data driven – and people, rather than the real flesh and blood they are, become numbers to financial folks and little more than sheep to be herded by the marketing people.

The value is created in reality – where people and products are actual and tangible - in engineering and manufacturing activities, and too often the leadership of the big companies is comprised of people with little or no experience, knowledge or appreciation for those disciplines.

Roger Smith, the CEO of General Motors, came from accounting and finance and, in fact, never worked a day in a GM factory. He is largely blamed for sending GM hurtling down the path that inevitably resulted in their bankruptcy as he poured billions into robots – the epitome of dehumanization - in a foolish strategy to compete with Toyota's focus on real people and real customers, and billions more into mergers and acquisitions and restructuring. What he never focused on, and seemingly never really understood, were cars and the people who make them and drive them – and GM's reality of how they are designed and how they are made. And this is typical.

In contrast the leaders of the successful companies, if they didn't come from the design or production background, sure spend most of their time there.

Wall Street serves a necessary purpose and there are most certainly many, many highly principled people who go to work in the investment and banking communities every day. Far be it from me or anyone else to judge them. However, the very nature of the publicly traded firm is to pursue a set of goals that begin and end with money. Nothing necessarily wrong with that, but the company and employees driven by higher principles should clearly recognize that their different goals require different management techniques. There is very little in the lessons from the big firms, or the academic community that focuses on them, that is applicable to the privately held, faith and values driven company in the way of management practices.

CHAPTER 9: *People*

Just about all I have written is about people – either directly or indirectly – and that is for good reason. In the end, that is what life is all about. Our sense of right and wrong, and the teachings of every faith, revolve around our relationships with people; and Bob Chapman is so utterly correct when he says that at some point, when our lives are over, all that will matter is the manner in which our lives impacted the people around us.

Business is also about people and little else – the people who work for us and with us, the people we buy from and sell to, and the people who risk their time and treasure in the support of the business. The huge divide between lean thinking and what has evolved as more typical management is a divide in attitudes about people. Throughout the 1900's there was a wide gulf between the folks in management and the people paid by the hour on the factory floors and in the front lines. It was the heyday of unions and never ending conflict between management and labor. Those days are over, however, and the "enlightened" management the Pope referred to are those who understand that point.

The conflict between management and labor that shaped so many management practices were, in large measure, a self-fulfilling prophecy. When labor and management treated each other like the enemy it was inevitable that the other side reacted like an enemy. Each side served the other plenty of justifications to dig their heels in deeper. Which side was right and which was wrong no longer matters, however. The conflict is over and everyone won; but as we keep fighting that old war unnecessarily everyone is starting to lose.

Battling between management and labor is a luxury we can no longer afford. It found its motivation in the juggernaut of the American economy that was fueled by huge gains in science and technology, world wars that devastated Europe and Asia and minimized America's global competition, and a booming immigrant population that brought a great work ethic into the American melting pot.

The American economic pie was one that steadily grew at an amazing rate, and the battle between management and labor was over how that pie would be split up. There was always enough for everyone; no one was going to starve. The question was who was going to get fatter. The pie isn't getting bigger fast enough now. Foreign competition is here as Europe and Asia have finally and fully recovered, and the technologies being developed today are ones that facilitate foreign competition. We all need to be more concerned about getting back to increasing the size of the pie, rather than fighting over how to slice it up.

While traditional management and GAAP driven accounting reduce people to 'headcount', lean is a completely people centered business theory. What it comes down to is this:

Do you think people are basically lazy, selfish, dishonest and generally looking for ways to get something for nothing?

Or do you think they are basically good, fair, willing to work hard and driven to accomplish things to be proud of?

Of course there are no absolutes when it comes to people. They come from all sorts of backgrounds, and hold the entire gamut of values and motivations. Traditional management, however, generally holds the first view and as such, management is largely about control. The Human Resources function is typically reflective of that point of view. Such companies have detailed human resources policy manuals and make people decisions more out of legal considerations than human ones. From the moment an employee first steps onto the property until the day they leave they are treated as potential adversaries in court. They seem to think that every employee is secretly looking for a way to file a discrimination suit, and HR is tasked with developing a document trail that will assure the company will prevail when that day comes.

In sharp contrast, lean management assumes the best and is based on empowerment and trust. It makes all the difference in the world when problems are approached based on the assumption that the problem resulted from poorly designed processes, rather than poorly motivated or incompetent people.

Which side of the question people of faith – any faith – fall out on is crystal clear. Whether someone works in front of a machine on a factory floor or in an office is reflective of different career choices and most probably different educational choices. To make an assumption as to peoples' values, morality or work ethic based on their educational and career choices, however, goes against the grain of the teachings of every priest, rabbi, imam and minister alive.

Quite to the contrary, people with a solid spiritual foundation know in their hearts and souls that there is dignity in all work, and that everyone is worthy of deep respect. There is no room in their hearts for the arrogance that claims moral superiority based on job titles or a greater paycheck. This is why the folks working in lean organizations – companies that truly understand and practice lean in its cultural and managerial entirety – flourish. Work takes on a completely different level of fulfillment and enjoyment when it is done surrounded by people you respect, and who have great respect for you. The energy level and the can-do attitude within lean companies is palpable when people work in an environment of mutual respect and accomplishment.

This is not to say that lean companies are Pollyannaish about people. They are well aware of the facts that many people do not share their values and way of working – most people do, but not all. In a lean organization a person's cultural fit trumps his or her technical skills and numerical results, and this is a huge departure for most companies.

Decades of HR theory have been devoted to ways of boiling people down to numbers for assessment purposes. Silly concepts such as 'You can't manage what you can't measure' and that anything important can and should be measured have driven managers to often ridiculous lengths to find ways of hanging numbers on people. Our preoccupation with accounting and metrics has resulted in putting extraordinary pressure on making numbers, rather than doing good things, if a person is to be given a raise, a bonus, or a promotion.

As a means of providing structure, a number of lean companies use a grid such as this one. They generally categorize a person on the X Axis; then the person's knowledge and experience are plotted on the Y Axis.

The objective is to provide a valuable insight into the areas in which people should develop, and to identify the people who can best lead the organization through the culture.

Discrete numbers are unimportant; what matters is the overall picture the assessment presents. Those people in Quadrant 1 – high in knowledge and high in cultural fit - are put into leadership positions and tasked with developing the people on their teams.

People in Quadrant 2 – high in cultural attributes but low in technical knowledge and skills - are targeted for training and education. They are viewed as the folks who represent the future of the company and well worth any investment in teaching them the tools of the trade.

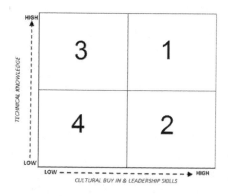

The people in Quadrant 3 are the people who may put up good numbers but do so in a manner that is often divisive, demeaning and confrontational. In a traditional organization that places huge value on numbers they are often promoted. In lean companies they are given coaching and a bit of time to shape up, or they are 'assisted in finding employment in a company that better suits their personalities' to paraphrase one very effective lean leader.

It is in how these people are dealt with that determines the true culture of the company. If the Quadrant 3 people are allowed to continue in positions of influence then the rest of the organization gets the loud and clear message that culture doesn't really matter. The high powered companies, however, know that culture is everything and these people must either change or leave, no longer allowing them to be a cancer on the organization.

The idea that the important aspects of the people in the company can be measured and that people can be ranked violates everything we know about life if we are people of love and faith. Can anyone measure their spouses, sons or daughters? Not in any important aspect. It is equally defiant of common sense to think the people who work with and for us can be measured. To be sure, we can measure our kids' height and weight, take their body temperature and look at their report cards, but any parent knows that those things are measurements of superficial things and hardly indicative of the core of the child.

The way lean companies achieve a higher performing culture is primarily to hire for it. They don't hire nearly as often though. For one, their strong culture typically keeps employee turnover at levels far below companies that manage via policy manuals. For another, their continuous quest to eliminate non-value adding work generates a steady stream of people with time on their hands – the folks who used to waste their time. And their commitment to lifetime employment causes them to increase their staff only when they are sure they are ready to live up to that principle. When they do hire, it is first and foremost for attitude, personal values, work ethic and willingness to be a part of a team – perfectly willing to either lead or follow depending on what is needed by the team at the time.

A great example is another extraordinarily lean company that leads the way in just about everything I have described thus far in this book – including making a lot of money and continually growing far beyond rates that most of the publicly traded guys can even imagine – is West Paw Design, a manufacturer of pet products in Bozeman, Montana. Their owner and President, Spencer Williams, talks of looking for people who are eager to commit to *"mastery, autonomy and purpose"*. The purpose: Williams *"sees his work and the work of his company as part of a much greater purpose: creating social and environmental change through business."*

Their production lead described working at West Paw saying, *"My values are very in sync with the company values, which makes our decisions feel good and helps me sleep well at night knowing we are doing what is best for our people — both customers and employees — and the planet. I also love the team I get to work with."*

Their Chief Operating Officer, Kathleen Johnson, says that what it takes to be considered a good employee at West Paw boils down to, *"Act with Integrity, Be Accountable, Be Tenacious, Be Friendly, Be Healthy, Continually Improve and Create Value."*

The mandate Kathleen lays down is like all of lean – not too complicated, but certainly not easy. Lean employees are more often compensated for knowledge than anything else - certainly not destructive factors such as piecework that create dismal quality and enormous waste no matter what management says about its quality control and supply chain management; and certainly not based on seniority. The most valuable employee in the company is the one who can do the greatest number of jobs. That creates flexibility, enhances flow, enables people to be great problem solvers and empathetic with the rest of the folks in the company ... all very good things that turn genuine respect for people into the driver of great business results.

Companies like West Paw set all of the conventional business wisdom on its ear. They make good money manufacturing and selling consumer products that are made in the United States, paying folks a lot of money, worrying about things like eliminating things that don't create value for customers and paying much less attention to headcount.

The difference between West Paw Design, Barry-Wehmiller, ATC and most companies is leadership that has absolute faith in their principles. Said Spencer Williams of his complete lack of formal business education when he started out (he has a degree in German of all things), *""I knew that I could solve the problems that came to me, and I didn't need a traditional education."* It was his faith in his innate knowledge of what makes sense, and what is right and wrong that drove him. The same is true of all of the incredibly successful lean companies. Principles trump accounting every time, and they keenly understand that.

Said one lean CEO, *"Companies are just collections (teams) of people trying to outperform other collections of people to satisfy a set of Customers.*" The companies with the best people working together on the best teams are the winners, and putting the best people into the best teams is done by principled leaders, not on the basis of accounting parameters.

CHAPTER 10: *A Few Specifics*

I did not want this to be either an in depth theological tome, nor did I wish to reinvent the wheel by getting into the details of Lean Management and Lean Accounting – both are subjects that have been treated very well by others. (And I have provided a solid list of resources on Lean at the end of the book.) That said, however, it will be helpful to hang at least a little meat on these bare bones and offer up a few examples of how these companies actually achieve such superior profits.

To completely understand lean thinking there are two basic ideas – both radically different from conventional business economic thinking and both very powerful – to be explained:

1. Price - Profit = Cost

2. The Black Box of Management Processes

The first is an inversion of conventional cost plus thinking. While many companies talk a good game the fact is that their basic economic model is COST + PROFIT = PRICE. You know this is true when you hear the word 'margin' bandied about until most are tired of hearing it. The context is most often in discussing the difference between the selling price of individual items and the standard, or fully absorbed cost. Prices are set based on some amount above the standard cost, and then tweaked to accommodate competition and other strategic considerations.

Lean thinking takes a different course. The price for your product is not up to you. The markets – the customers – and the level of value you create for them sets the prices. The price you come up with as a result of some cost based arithmetic is completely irrelevant.

And unless you are running a charity, profit is not optional or variable either. What you do control – and the only truly controllable variable – is your cost. So we start with the prices

Converting the company away from treating hourly folks as headcount and a variable cost to be manipulated in order to optimize costs is a little like taking the 'Cortez Approach'.

Legend has it that when Cortez arrived from Spain with some 500 or so Conquistadors near the modern Mexican city of Veracruz he ordered his ships to be burned to the waterline. This was to cut off any possible retreat for his men when the going inevitably got tough. They would have no choice but to be tough and creative and come up with another solution for survival other than to turn around and sail home to Spain.

Likewise, lean leaders see laying off employees as an ethically unacceptable – and intellectually lazy – solution to business problems. They simply take that option off the table and task management with getting creative and coming up with another solution.

That creative, different solution beginning with a directive that cutting their way out of problems is not one of the options. This leaves growing the business as the only alternative. It results in increasing the flow of product across the fixed base of people.

needed to (1) achieve your market strategy, and (2) to fully utilize your capacity.

From that total sales volume we then deduct the direct material costs, and the total cost of your labor. Note that we are not particularly interested in this on a unit basis. We are pricing holistically, and looking at sales minus direct material at the value stream level, or sometimes at the company or plant level if there is only one value stream.

The second principle – the 'Black Box' approach – is a radical departure from standard costing. Standard costing is the bane of profitable manufacturing. Popular because standard costs are the tool for valuing inventory and achieving GAAP's requirement for full absorption and compliance with something called the Matching Principle (these are the nefarious accounting practices that create the illusion of inventory being a good thing), they actually cause non-value adding overhead expenses to be diffused and spread out into such minute pieces as to be almost invisible. Rather than allocate them and make decisions at the individual product cost level, lean companies keep them isolated and separate from the core manufacturing processes where they can be attacked.

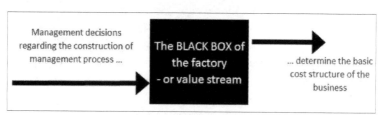

The manufacturing processes are essentially within a black box. How quality and the supply chain, for instance, are to be managed is something management has decided independent of those processes.

If the math doesn't work out when subtracting the direct materials, labor cost (which is treated as fixed) and the cost of all of the management processes, then management must make different decisions regarding the construction of all of the non-value adding support processes.

There are basically two different ways of attacking the cost structure: Kaizen and kaikaku. Kaizen, as previously mentioned, is continuous improvement, while kaikaku is a more radical approach. According to Wikipedia, *"Kaikaku (Japanese for 'radical change') is a business concept concerned with making fundamental and radical changes to a production system, unlike Kaizen which is focused on incremental minor*

The notion of waste is a recurring theme in lean and throughout this book, and it is described as anything the customer will not pay for. A good way to understand it is to consider two nearly identical items on the shelf at Walmart – one costs $5 and the other costs $6. If you could ask the manufacturer of the $6 item what the additional dollar is for, if they were to answer, "It is to pay for our ERP system", or for the cost of more material handling, warehousing, shipping, advertising, meetings or packaging you would most likely opt for the $5 item. On the other hand if they answered that it is for superior materials that will make the product last longer or deliver more consistent performance then you may be inclined to opt for the $6 item.

A frequent mistake is for managers to think that because costs are perceived to be 'necessary' they are value adding or at least unavoidable. Lean thinkers see them as necessary only within the current management process structure – change the basic management processes and they are no longer necessary. This is the essence of kaikaku.

---

changes. Both Kaizen and Kaikaku can be applied to activities other than production."

Put another way, if the support process is basically the way management wants the process to be executed, it will be left in place and the people working in the process will be tasked with slowly but steadily wringing the cost and defects from the process, continually improving it. If overall costs are way out of line, however, or if the process is overly complicated, costly or difficult to execute properly, management may opt to simply blow it up and look for a creative alternative.

The juiciest targets for operating with a radically lower cost structure than most companies are just about anything the traditional managers do on a computer – and ERP systems are the prime target. It is not that lean companies are opposed to information technology; rather, it is that they see the need for information to flow in a much different way. And they see big IT systems as creators of significant levels of non-value adding waste.

ERP systems create the need for planners, production schedulers, cost accountants and buyers. They require data collection and entry, as well as supervisors to oversee all of this, along with the costs of the software and hardware itself.

ATC doesn't use ERP at all nor does West Paw Design, while many are systematically dismantling their old legacy ERP systems. McCloskey International in Ontario, Canada schedules their production and executes their supply chain in manufacturing extremely complex rock crushing machines with magnetic boards and kanban cards in the plant, achieving shorter lead times and greater inventory turns than their competitors by a wide margin. Anchor Tent blows the doors off of their competition with incredibly short lead times and far less inventory in a highly seasonal business with little more than kanban cards and an Excel spreadsheet to plan and optimize capacity.

Some lean companies use the bare bones of an ERP system for accounting purposes, largely because it can serve as a handy data base, but they don't use it for supply chain execution.

What enables them to take millions of dollars out of their costs structures is mostly their culture. They see capturing information on the factory floor, using IT to send that information to someone sitting in an office somewhere – a scheduler or a buyer, for instance – and then having that person tell the floor what to do next as a colossal waste of time and money. In their view the information flow should be from wherever the information arose to wherever it is needed, without detouring for someone else's review or approval. If there are any decisions to be made about the data, the operators creating or using the data can be trained to make them.

I have used the term 'kanban' to describe their approach. Technically, kanban is a Japanese term meaning something like 'display card'. In lean companies it has evolved to generally describe just about any method to communicate the need to replenish something. Lean companies operate on a demand pull basis, rather than sophisticated forecasting models. Under this approach, they set a minimal inventory level in place and their purchasing and production simply replenish that which has been used to meet actual customer demand – 'Sell one, make one; sell two, make two, etc...' This keeps their factories and supply chain in perfect synchronization with customer demand.

Kanban, or demand pull, can take a variety of forms, including returnable containers – when a bin or box of parts is used, the bin is returned to the supplier and that bin is all the signal the supplier needs to fill the bin and send it back. At ATC one piece of paper goes back and forth between their plant and their tire supplier, progressively filled out as it goes between them, and that one piece of paper replaces purchase orders, shipping documents, receiving records and invoices. At the end of each month the document goes to ATC accounting, which pays the supplier for everything that was shipped during the month and a new piece of paper begins its journey. No computers, no duplication, no matching up of three documents in order to pay an invoice, and massively less time spent on the administrative effort of doing very repetitive work.

In these companies forecasting still takes place, but it tends to be at a fairly high level and is primarily for planning capacity, as well as to let suppliers know what their capacity requirements will be. They don't actually buy or make much of anything to the forecast. Some of them use a technique called Level Loaded Demand Pull to flatten factory demand in the face of a highly seasonal business. Just about all of them have unique wrinkles they put into their processes to accommodate the particular nuances of their environment.

Similar approaches are taken in accounting, quoting, quality control and the rest of their basic management processes. The common theme is that they have mapped the process, trained and empowered the people working within the process, and set everyone to the task of coming up with eliminating steps and cutting delay and cost from them. The various lean conferences, such as the one held by AME – the Association for Manufacturing Excellence that draws thousands of attendees every year – is normally little more than a sharing of the myriad creative ways in which lean companies have conjured up unique alternatives to traditional, labor intensive management processes.

Perhaps the biggest reason lean companies avoid systems such as ERP is their cultural aversion to complexity. Complexity is the enemy of short cycle time, and it is the enemy of continuous improvement. When McCloskey has an idea for improvement they can have their magnetic boards and kanban cards modified in a matter of hours. When Anchor has a better idea, their spreadsheets can be modified and cards changed in the same day. ERP centered companies, however, put their improvement idea on a waiting list for their IT folks or the software supplier to make the change, and the time it takes to make such changes is typically measured in months.

The other cultural bugaboo that complex IT solutions create is the reinforcement of ivory towers – headquarters staff folks who do not add value for customers but amass power and control due largely to establishing themselves as the only people who really understand these systems. They too often turn themselves into vital people in any decision making with little accountability and little real knowledge of factory floor problems and conditions. A cultural bias toward simplicity tends to preclude such overhead pockets and improvement logjams from arising.

CHAPTER 11: *Taking Action*

A few years ago my youngest son, Andy, accompanied me on a cross country trip from Chicago to Tacoma for my daughter's wedding. Andy and I were tasked with driving and hauling the load of stuff weddings require while the rest of the family flew out west. Along the way we stopped at West Paw Design to say hello and see how things were going. The visit lasted no more than a half hour, and it is important to note that my college age son knew little about lean and nothing about manufacturing. But after that visit his reaction was to ask if I could help him get a job at West Paw when he finished school. He didn't care what they did or what the job was. He simply knew he wanted to be a part of the energy and the atmosphere. The difference between West Paw and every other business Andy had seen was visceral and powerful.

That is always the way when someone visits these truly lean companies. When people have the opportunity to contribute to an organization that supports their values – makes a genuine commitment to making people's lives and the community better - and empowers everyone to contribute to the creative work needed to overcome the inevitable problems encountered along the way they not only work hard but have a lot of fun. You cannot help but want to be a part of it.

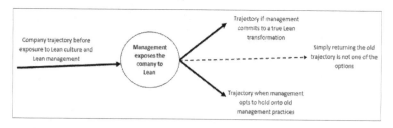

Leadership should be forewarned of the consequences of exposing the company to lean thinking, lean culture and the opportunity align the values good people have with their work. The company will never be the same afterwards.

If management embraces the opportunity then amazing things start to happen; but when management explores lean, and opts to maintain the status quo, the best people in the company are very likely to leave. It happens quite often and the company may well be left with the people who are less driven by the excitement and opportunity to be a part of something big, while the people who represent the best potential leadership in the long term move to other jobs where they can follow through with the challenge and joy of lean. And of course that is the way it works. When people have experiences like my son's; or when they see how things are done at ATC, or they observe the management practices and the cultural atmosphere at Barry-Wehmiller they will never settle for siloed, headcount centered management again.

Just about everyone comes to lean in the same way. They assume that management is basically sound – that accounting is inherently correct, that functional organizations are the only way to set things up, that ERP systems are logical and that labor efficiency is very, very important. It doesn't even dawn on them to question these things, as if the text for the Management 101 book was inscribed on the reverse side of the tablets Moses hauled down from Mount Sinai. With management unquestioned, people see lean as a set of tools and techniques largely only relevant to the shop floor; and they apply them within the old framework as devices to reduce cost – especially labor cost. The result is a shop floor that looks a little better, but no real impact on the bottom line. And, of course there is no impact for the simple reason that nothing about lean was designed to reduce labor costs in the manner in which traditional managers measure it.

At that point, if senior management was involved much in the first place they pretty much check out. Some deciding that lean doesn't work – often hiding behind the claim that 'We're different', sometimes labeling lean as just another over-hyped fad. If they address culture at all it is in the form of an effort to get the people on the shop floor involved in conjuring up ideas for their own demise.

Many, however, claim success – asserting that they are now a 'lean company'. You will hear them use phrases such as 'We implemented lean', as if it were a new bit of software. It was a project with a beginning and an end, and the effort is now complete. With that behind them the managers can get back to what they were doing before, casting about for the next improvement project to be conquered.

It is not entirely management's fault. There are hordes of consultants out there and shelves full of books suggesting that's all there is to lean, but it fails a common sense test. You get what you manage. Manage the company the same way you did in the past and it is inevitable that you will get the same results you did in the past. You can't change the basic trajectory of the business unless you change how you manage it. If that weren't true, why would we need management at all?

The gut wrenching, radical transformation in the business is not on the shop floor – it is in the management offices. If everyone in management is looking at the same accounting information, the same ERP output, sitting in the same meetings with the same relationships with the same people, guess what? They will make the same decisions. And those decisions will keep the company on the same path.

But most of the successful lean leaders don't come to this enlightened approach to management through such logic. They come to it through their principles. They don't care if the body of knowledge is called lean or much of anything else. They are not pursuing lean for lean's sake, or because they are looking for Toyota-like, long term profits. They come to it in search of a way to manage by their principles. Then they see the likes of Barry-Wehmiller, ATC, West Paw and Wahl Clipper. They see people working in harmony with their faith, and being extraordinarily successful along the way. And then they are hooked.

The starting point is almost always a senior leader, or a leadership team, that is determined to find a more humane, inclusive way to run the business. They feel a deep sense of genuine love and responsibility for the people involved in the business and, through lean, they find a way to turn those principles into a successful business. Lean cannot teach principles to unprincipled managers, but the basic human principles derived from faith are what enable managers to see and be drawn to the power of lean.

So the principled leader is not content with the basic shop floor tools. The ones I have cited are like pit bulls who keep challenging, questioning and digging. They delve deeper and deeper into lean to find the core of the management structures and philosophies needed to allow them to manage by their principles; and they dive even deeper into the core of lean culture until they fully understand and support the cultural rules needed to turn the whole company into one driven by the leader's strongly held beliefs.

This is the challenge this book presents. If the reader is such a principled leader and looking for a better way, then it is time to take that deep dive and to take on that pit bull-like tenacity. The promise of this book is that, if you do so, you will find a relatively obscure but well-trodden path to follow. It is the path the likes of Bob Chapman, Steve Brenneman and Kiichiro Toyoda have walked. It's not an easy path, but it leads to where you want to go.

And if the reader is a middle manager, an engineer, a supply chain professional and you are not working in an environment that not only accepts your faith and principles, but encourages you to build and act on them, then you need to take a long, hard look at who is running things. If that person is a person of faith and principles then your task is to give them this book, to help them see the path, and to encourage them to take that deep dive. But if they are not such a person, then get out – now – while the getting is good.

There are hundreds, probably thousands, of companies like those described that can provide you with an opportunity to live like the man from West Paw who said, *"My values are very in sync with the company values, which makes our decisions feel good and helps me sleep well at night knowing we are doing what is best for our people — both customers and employees — and the planet. I also love the team I get to work with."*

There is no reason why everyone should not have what he has.

CHAPTER 12: *Start Learning*

I hope that by now, if I haven't convinced you I have at least piqued your curiosity. Either way, the next step is to learn. A lean transformation is nothing short of a complete overhaul of how you think – how you think about management and your career. It requires a completely different understanding of accounting and how the company makes money. The real objective of learning more, however, is to give you confidence that, if you simply start making decisions and taking action based on your beliefs and principles rather than the traditional approach to business you were taught, things will work out.

In advocating lean you are apt to hear its proponents suggesting that a leap of faith is required. There is some truth in this, at least to the extent that people of principles routinely take leaps of faith, taking actions that are not easy or the ones most other people might take. That is what principles are all about. But leaps of faith are not the same as leaps of logic.

Lean management, culture and manufacturing are very logical – the bits and pieces all fit together in a very logical, functioning machine. This book is primarily aimed at making that point – that there is a logical, economically powerful way to run a business that is consistent with those things that make up the better angels of your nature. The learning process required to go forward is to see and understand each of those bits and pieces, and to understand how the whole, integrated machine fits together.

The leap of faith required is the same as the leap of faith you take when you act as the spiritual head of your family, making decisions and setting a course that does not necessarily make the kids happy but you know will better serve them in the long run. You trust that, by insisting that they do the right thing, it will pay off.

This is the leap of faith needed for a CEO to sit his or her staff down and tell them that, even though the company may be profitable and they are enjoying a sense of security, the whole thing just doesn't sit right with you and you are going to take the company down a radically different path. You can do this if you have a conviction that it can never be a mistake to do the right thing according to your faith and beliefs.

And it is the leap of faith an individual might make, and ask his or her spouse to make, when he sits her down and says that, even though the XYZ Megacorp pays well and provides a lucrative career path, he can no longer rationalize a professional life that feels so wrong; and he is going to change jobs to a smaller, less secure company because it is being led according to principles he can support and that enable him to know that he is better serving God's purpose for his life.

So where does this education start? Any number of places. There are many books, videos, seminars and gatherings; and consultants galore – so many, in fact, that the problem can be one of separating the wheat from the chaff. While this list is nowhere near complete, I can offer a few such sources that I know to be highly credible and provided by people who work in lean as much because of their passion for the inherent goodness of it as they do as the source of their paychecks.

LEI – The Lean Enterprise Institute is the organization created by Jim Womack. Jim is now somewhat retired but his organization is still going full force. Jim Womack is generally viewed as the man who coined the term lean when he co-authored *The Machine That Changed the World* some 25 years ago. His organization provides a wide range of training and educational resources, all of which are first class. Their emphasis is on the broader concepts and underlying philosophies of lean, as well as the complete range of tools and techniques used to transform the company.

Lean Frontiers – Lean Frontiers is the organization created by Jim Huntzinger and Dwayne Butcher, both men of great faith and integrity, to put together the first Lean Accounting Summit in 2005. The Summit is still an annual event, along with a number of other Summits Lean Frontiers organizes. They tend to focus on management processes, including HR, Design, employee development, IT and others, along with Lean Accounting. All of their events are very well organized and have excellent content.

The Gemba Academy – The Gemba Academy specializes in online and video training and has hundreds of training tools that cover most of the lean waterfront. They focus most on lean tools and techniques, as well as lean culture.

The Kaizen Institute – The Kaizen Institute is a global company with training and consulting offices throughout the world. They are an excellent resource, especially in the areas of lean tools and techniques, supply chain, and culture.

Lean Accounting:

In the area of Lean Accounting, Brian Maskell's BMA and Jean Cunningham are two widely recognized authorities. Brian's book, *Practical Lean Accounting*, and Jean's book *Real Numbers* (written with Orrie Fiume, another highly regarded expert) are two of the best and most popular.

Jerry Solomon, Larry Grasso, Frances Kennedy and Nick Katko are also excellent resources.

Lean Culture:

Two books rise to the level of 'must read' in order to understand the culture and people aspect of lean. Mike Rother's *Toyota Kata* and *Creating a Kaizen Culture* by Jon Miller and Mike Wroblewski.

Lean Leadership & Principles:

There are a couple of books that also rise to the level of 'must read' especially for senior managers who need to understand lean in its broadest, most comprehensive terms. First and foremost among them is Jeff Liker's *The Toyota Way*.

Additional essential books include the late Eli Goldratt's *The Goal; Seeing the Whole Value Stream* by Jim Womack and Dan Jones; *Lean Thinking* by Jim Womack and Dan Jones; and Jamie Flinchbaugh's *The Hitchhiker's Guide to Lean: Lessons from the Road*.

This is by no means a comprehensive list, but it is a list of books that have taught me much, written by people I hold in very high regard. You can't go wrong with this list, and by seeking your education from the organizations I have mentioned.

Lean Companies – The best learning resource are the lean companies themselves. No matter what part of the world you are in, you can find them; and it is almost universally true that they are willing to open their doors and share. That seems to be a hallmark of lean organizations. Seek them out and ask your peers what they know, what they have done, and what advice they can give.

A final note to the reader:

A particular thank you is owed to Steve Brenneman of ATC, Bob Chapman from Barry-Wehmiller, Jim Huntzinger at Lean Frontiers, Jon Miller with the Gemba Academy, and Stacey Scott from West Paw Design for the time they so freely gave in assisting me with this book. Thanks, as well, to all of the outstanding lean leaders I have been privileged to meet throughout the last 30 years who have taught and inspired me.

Thank you readers for sticking with my book all the way to the end. I hope my passion for lean has shown through my writing. Lean has provided me with the means to make a good living and to provide for my family, but more important, it has provided me with incredible joy. I have had many experiences in which the positive potential of lean and my small contribution to it have impacted people in a big way, and no one can ask more from a profession than that.

I sincerely hope there is something in my writing that has touched or inspired you to take the next step. I stand ready and willing to help you in any way I can.

Best wishes on your lean journey, and may God bless you along the way.

Bill Waddell ~ 2015

Made in the USA
Middletown, DE
21 March 2016